POW Survival in the Philippines and Japan

CAPTURED HONOR

BOB WODNIK

Washington State University Press
Pullman, Washington

WASHINGTON STATE UNIVERSITY

Washington State University Press
PO Box 645910
Pullman, Washington 99164-5910
Phone: 800-354-7360
Fax: 509-335-8568
E-mail: wsupress@wsu.edu
Web site: wsupress.wsu.edu

Library of Congress Cataloging-in-Publication Data

Wodnik, Bob, 1954-
    Captured honor : POW survival in the Philippines and Japan / Bob Wodnik.
        p. cm.
    Includes bibliographical references and index.
    ISBN 0-87422-260-5 (pbk. : alk. paper)
        1. World War, 1939-1945—Prisoners and prisons, Japanese. 2. Prisoners of
    war—United States—Biography. 3. Prisoners of war—Japan—History—20th
    century. 4. Prisoners of war—Philippines—History—20th century. I. Title.

D805.J3 W64 2003
940.54'7252'0922797—dc21   2002154210

WSU PRESS
Fine Quality Books from the Pacific Northwest

CAPTURED
HONOR

To Bridget and Erin

ACKNOWLEDGMENTS

*M*any people graciously opened their hearts and minds to relate their stories to me and make this book possible. U.S. Army and Marine Corps veterans of the Everett locality, who are among the principal personages of this story, included Jack Elkins, Odas Greer, Galen Martin, Fran Agnes, and Henry Chamberlain. All were prisoners of war under the Japanese in the Philippines and Japan.

Other former POWs sharing their memories included Larry Rathbun, a survivor of the Zentsuji Prison Camp on Shikoku Island, Japan, and Frank Gadwa, held in Stalag 17B in Germany.

Other Everett, Washington, residents who were part of the World War II generation and who have helped breathe life into this colorful era of the city's past include Paul and Dorothy Alley, Al and Irma Petershagen, Harry and Jenny Sissons, Carl and Jodi Gipson, Ross Hoaglund, Art De Rosa, Don Hoerner, Jim Tolnay, Richard Bold, Mike Hackler, Larry O'Donnell, and many others.

Dave Dilgard, historian from the Everett Public Library, shared a keen perspective on his hometown during this important period of its history.

Harry Dahl colored in the outlines of the life of his cousin, Ed Fox.

Sharon Salyer spent hours editing, encouraging, and advising.

To all, my deepest gratitude.

CONTENTS

ILLUSTRATIONS

MAIN PERSONAGES

Fran Agnes. Sergeant mechanic, 20th Pursuit Squadron, U.S. Army Air Corps. Captured on Bataan, April 1942; Bataan Death March survivor.

Henry Chamberlain. U.S. Army medic. Zero Ward at Cabanatuan; survived hell ship *Haro Maru*.

Jack Elkins. Private First Class, B Company, First Battalion, Fourth Marines. Captured on Corregidor; Yokohama POW #997.

Gracie Emmett. Everett bar girl; Ed Fox's wartime love.

Ed Fox. Bibliophile; night clerk at Everett's Strand Hotel.

Joe Gear. Left on a Yokohama dock to die; "See ya' on Market Street."

Odas Greer. Sergeant, Battery M, 60th Coast Artillery, U.S. Army. Survived wounds on Corregidor; Yokohama POW #725.

Jerry Hanson. USMC. Jack Elkins' buddy; Yokohama POW #995.

Fred Johannsen. Orphaned when a child. Jack Elkins' buddy; Yokohama Prisoner #996.

Galen Martin. Sergeant, Battery C, 60th Coast Artillery, U.S. Army. Captured on Corregidor; forced to work in Japanese copper mines.

Roy A. Wederbrook. USMC. Died in his machine gun nest on Corregidor; "Ain't backin' up no further."

1

Tell us your story
(October 1945)

*T*HERE WAS THIS AUTUMN EVENING not long after he'd returned home when Jack Elkins found himself fidgeting alongside other returned servicemen on a wood planked stage.

The hometown crowd wanted stories; nice packaged tales where heroes beat long odds. They wanted blood without splatters. They wanted death from a distance. They wanted Hollywood actors dying dignified and intact on a huge movie screen while the audience ate popcorn and held hands in the dark.

Jack's face burned. The man in the small town suit facing a big chrome microphone turned towards him. The suit mocked Jack, leered at him, was everything he'd come to dread about home.

Run, run, as far as you can, as fast as you can, and never look back!

"C'mon up to the microphone, son. Tell us all about it."

So that was it. It was for *him* they were doing all this; it was for *him* they organized this "Welcome Home Servicemen" night.

Tell us all about it, Jack. Tell us how many Nips you killed on that Philippine beachhead. Tell us how forever in your mind bright blue Manila Bay is stained with red Japanese blood. Blood, by the way, from your own Springfield rifle that parted the wind-tossed creeper grass when fired from the hillside above. Those Japanese soldiers had parents, didn't they, and yes, hometowns too, in case anyone cared.

He tried sneaking off to a chair furthest from the microphone, but persistent hands reached for him; mouths coaxed and cajoled him back towards the center where everyone could eyeball a piece of him. And that's where he sat dejected and alone while their stares penetrated right through to his heart.

There was his grammar school principal, the hardware store clerk, old high school girlfriends, and the man who pumped gasoline into the family car.

They wanted to see if it was Jack Elkins, high school quarterback, or some sanitarium freak returned home to mom and dad. He'd never forget the look from his father when he first drove home from the Army hospital and pulled into the driveway, that surreptitious check-out to make sure his son was still all there. His dad thought Jack hadn't noticed, but he had. Jack saw everything with eyes that betrayed nothing.

Time hadn't stood still while he wasted away in a Japanese prison camp. His high school girlfriend had married a close friend, not that that mattered much now. And that first night home when it was finally time for bed, his sister and another one of his friends climbed together to an upstairs bedroom. They too had married while he was gone.

Now every one of those 600 faces in the church auditorium wanted a part of him. It grew insufferably hot and still those faces stared. His family was there, his mother—his good faithful mother who wrote him letters every Sunday that he never saw. She mailed packages of dried prunes, hard candies, chocolate, noodles, coffee, and tea that lined the bellies of Japanese guards.

When word came that Japan surrendered, his young brother and sister ran across the street to the Baptist church and rang the bell, over and over so hard that the bell rope broke and his sister fell laughing to the steeple floor.

"C'mon over, Jack," beckoned the man in the suit. "Lean into the microphone."

So that was it. Relax now son and tell us your story is what he meant. Tell us about Walsh and Gaskin, who slept a few feet away in your lice infested Yokohama prison camp. Tell us how they shared food when there was extra, how they looked out for each other, how they celebrated their birthdays with a little hoarded rice.

Put us alongside you in camp that day in Kamaishi near the end of the war when the American battlewagon in the blue-green harbor opened up, shelling the nearby Japanese steel mill for more than two hours. Details, details. Paint for us how the whole forward deck of the USS *Massachusetts* lit up with flames and black smoke, and then five, six, seven seconds later shells whistled so close overhead it was as if you could reach up and let them slip through your fingers before they exploded into the buildings.

Explain how Gaskin and the others dove into a shelter, but you, because you had some sixth sense about such things, ran towards the bay carrying only your trusty blanket. And there you lay in that rocky ditch before your prison barracks, hearing those shells crying overhead in the mid-span of a hot summer afternoon.

Describe how an American shell, one of our very own, hit the POW shelter near the steel foundry and Gaskin died quick while his buddy Walsh was away on work detail. Tell us how you watched one prisoner after another come screaming out of that shelter chased by red-yellow flames licking at their clothes. Remember how a few days later one of those prisoners died, the skin on his blistered back and arms crawling with white maggots. Remember it all and let us savor the details. Tell us how three hundred of you walked into the mountains that night to sleep on the hardwood floor of a bombed-out schoolhouse. It rained, remember, and two grimy prisoners shared your blanket, bone cold all of you.

The next morning Walsh begged to return and cremate the dead down at the steel mill, mostly his buddy Gaskin. Everyone knew, didn't they, that that was the last thing you did for a friend. You laid his soul to rest and maybe a little of your own as well.

But they forgot to tell you that over there stories never had a Hollywood ending.

So Walsh waited in the courtyard of the school along with everyone else that morning when the high-octane whine of an American plane skimmed through the sunshine. A second plane hissed right behind with a bomb that exploded several hundred feet away. It was a wild random shot, completely ridiculous except that it tore out a chunk of concrete the size of a cantaloupe and sent it hurtling through the sunlight.

It must've been god-sent, that deadly piece of rock, how else do you explain why it picked out Walsh, and only Walsh, from the three hundred others standing in that courtyard.

And then it was Walsh they loaded on that small wood cart and it was his body they lugged down the hillside, where it was cremated alongside Gaskin. Walsh and Gaskin, Gaskin and Walsh, together again.

The church audience waited, sizing him up like his father had that first day back. You either tell them everything, or you tell them nothing.

Tell them about the forever tomorrows of a Japanese prison camp. Tell them what it's like bathing once every two weeks in water tepid and filthy from the stink of dozens before. Describe what it meant sleeping on a hard cold board with two cocooned blankets and the same tired thoughts rattling inside your head.

You either tell all, or you tell nothing.

"Give them credit," Jack whispered into the big chrome microphone, his eyes searching out his parents. "They sent me off in good shape."

And then he sat down—and spent most of his life trying to forget.

2

Don't stop, don't look
(Philippines, 1942)

*T*HE SNIPERS WERE IMPOSSIBLE. Their painted hands and faces melted into the green Nipa frond jungle until they were part of it. It was the way of the warrior, or maybe something else not quite human. Crack. One rifle shot a day, every day. Find me if you can.

Army Air Corps Private Fran Agnes crouched among them deep in the jungle's aorta, feeling their eyes, smelling the hot stagnant air, expecting a bullet to lay him flat.

Sure there was danger in this miserable place, but there was living too, and a plodding sense of duty. And so for weeks after the jungle changed them in ways they'd yet to discover, he and his young Army mates continued to plunder the parts from airplane skeletons scattered about like greasy bones. You used everything like you ate everything, wasting nothing—men truly lost.

In their scrounging one day, they stumbled across some leftover carbine rifles and saucer-shaped doughboy helmets that they slipped down over their sweaty brows. After that they were the Flying Infantry—outwitting the jungle with carbines and wrenches. A laugh.

But the Japanese could be anywhere. He felt their cold eyes through the thick trees and ropy vines. The air was alive like the inside of an arboretum, with those eyes watching, always those eyes.

Occasionally a shot broke from the underbrush and an unsuspecting American, an officer more often than not, crumpled onto the jungle floor. One a day, every day, origin unknown.

Bataan, on the mosquito-infested Filipino island of Luzon, was an awful place to fight a war. It began with malaria and hunger and the hopeless feeling of being cutoff and abandoned. And then it got worse.

At first, after the Japanese army attacked the huge bustling city of Manila and pushed out the Allied troops, the Bataan Peninsula with its mountain range, gullies, streams, and ravines too numerous to count and too deep to cross, had seemed a good place to settle in for a defensive struggle. Just three weeks after the war began in December 1941, nearly 80,000 troops evacuated Manila and slipped into the jungle. About 13,000 of those troops were Americans, the rest Filipino Army. But in their hurry they failed to cart in enough food and medicine—so by early January all were eating half rations and hungry constantly. An army without food and medicine soon isn't an army.

Fran and the Flying Infantry stretched their dwindling supplies of rice and tinned salmon with anything that moved. The sinewy carabao, or water buffalo, tasted like mud. Lizards, parrots, and snakes, grotesque in every way, were tossed in pots of boiling water. Some ate monkey, turning in revulsion from the animal's child-like hands. In four months' time Fran lost forty-percent body weight off a wiry frame that had little extra to start with.

Even that would've been bearable had there been real hope that reinforcements carrying food and medicine would arrive from across the ocean to help pound the Japanese off Bataan and back into the South China Sea. But most of America's Pacific fleet battleships lay on the bottom of Pearl Harbor and the troops knew they were alone. One morning in particular told Fran how it would end.

The rattle of a patched-together American P40, flying low overhead on that steamy jungle morning, spread some sense of security, a little faith, if you will, over the wilderness below.

But it couldn't last because it wasn't true. Truth came from a Japanese Zero, which appeared suddenly across the perfect blue. The Zero was everything the American plane wasn't. It was everywhere at once, barely touching the sky as if riding a breath of wind. The Japanese patrolled the air over the Philippines with brutal precision. It was theirs, they had won it. Not that they found much competition ever since America's best fighters had been squandered on the runways of Clark and Nichols fields not far from Manila.

Fran squinted through a clearing up into a brilliant sky. The two planes circled warily, diving and feigning as if boxers in a fight's first rounds. The preliminaries continued for some time until the veteran Japanese pilot grew tired of the game.

The creaky American warplane was no match for a Zero with its two 20 mm cannon and oiled machine guns that confidently tat-tatted across the blue. It was embarrassing and over quickly. Given equal equipment, it would've been a fight. As it was, the American pilot soon bailed from his dying aircraft. The Zero lazily banked into the glare of the sun and then back around again, until it was over the wisp of smoke where the crippled P40 had disappeared into the jackfruit and creeper vines. The killing would be unhurried.

Floating softly, much too softly, the American pilot jerked his mushroom white parachute, and then again, as if willing himself into the green tree tops, their limbs spread in welcome and rising two hundred feet in places.

But there was no hurrying the parachute that simply drifted in its own slow, agonizing way until the Zero was on it. Tat-a-tat, tat-a-tat, tat-a-tat. Fran turned away. The parachute continued drifting, the American now dead weight against the harness webbing.

Before the business with the Japanese turned ugly, Fran was a second class Army aircraft mechanic and proud of it, pulling down $72 a month, with three meals a day and a cot thrown in the package free and clear.

He lived at Clark Field north of Manila in the mechanic's quarters, built at the edge of a jungle near the apron where B17 Flying Fortress bombers and speedy P40 fighters were serviced.

Army Air Corps life was OK. There were training and drills and, when you had your fill, more training and more drills. But the mechanics were proud of their work. They stood and watched the big noisy planes taxi down the runway and float up over the thick canopy of Lauan trees, until they disappeared into that Philippine sky. Fran knew that if it hadn't been for the mechanics with engine grease smearing their coveralls, those starched Army pilots wouldn't be flying anywhere. Sometimes he watched until all that was left of those airplanes was the faintest farewell drone. It was the engines talking and any good mechanic understood their complaints and satisfactions, the chatter of well tuned machinery.

Fran was barely 20 years old, but the face staring back at him in his barracks' mirror was that of a man. Full grown at last and without the lines of worry and hunger that would soon peck at him.

Seldom now did his mind drift back to when he picked apples for a quarter an hour in a sunny Wenatchee, Washington, orchard. One thing was certain: he'd never become a college boy on those wages, even if he were the best red apple picker in Douglas County, which he wasn't.

A cousin had joined the Army Air Corps and was soon sporting around the streets of Wenatchee in a bright, new Ford roadster. There was money to be made elsewhere, Fran could see that. So one day in 1940, just after he'd finished high school, he climbed resolutely down the old wood ladder that leaned against a gnarled arm of an apple tree and found himself inside the Wenatchee post office, where an Army Air Corps recruiter waited with the keys to a fleet of roadsters, if not dreams even bigger.

In that way he was typical of young men tested by the Great Depression and anxious to get on with life. Many knew war was coming, knew it sure as every newspaper headline. They had something to give, felt responsibility beyond their years, yet were painfully naive about what lay ahead.

The country was full of them, men who would look back on those early years with a certain kind of innocence—

Galen Martin was 20 years old, single, and roaming around the country in an old backcountry carnival when he and a buddy joined up in Corpus Christi, Texas.

"We had nothing to lose, just wanted some adventure," he'd later recall.

Henry Chamberlain had just pulled through the Great Depression as best he could, learning lessons that would serve him later.

Jack Elkins came all the way from the flats of Eastern Washington to join the Marines in Seattle on the day that the Tacoma Narrows Bridge, Gallopin' Gertie, blew down in a freak winter windstorm. If he'd been a young man who kept track of omens, that would've been one. As it was, he never made the connection. Not until much later.

No, all in all, Army life seemed OK when you considered all the possibilities. Good enough to start with anyway—the real part, the grownup part. Fran belonged to something now, something necessary and good.

He was dozing off on his Army cot in his stuffy mechanic's quarters near the Clark Field runway on December 8, 1941, when a voice outside thundered something about incoming, and, judging from the commotion, it was quite a show. The voice seemed elsewhere and everywhere at once, like a ventriloquist's trick.

Perhaps it was a new squad of B17s flying in with a bellyful of bluster to help defend the Philippine Islands. That meant more work for the mechanics, but the thought of extra protection felt good. He'd heard rumblings about the war-hungry Japanese from the moment he boarded the SS *Washington* after boot camp in California. Soon he'd see for himself. Following a layover in Hawaii, the liner continued to Japanese-occupied Shanghai, China, where the future revealed itself in murderous detail. One morning while anchored in the Wang Pu River, he happened to glance over the ship's railing. The sight sickened him. A stream of bloated Chinese bodies floated by on the morning tide.

Now it was several months later in the Philippines and Fran lay on his cot, resting in the tropical mid-day heat. The pilots were eating lunch in the Clark Field mess, their planes fueled and lined up slick as dominoes on the runway. Something about the growing intensity of the voices outside, however, startled him to action.

He hustled off his cot. Sure enough, there were planes up there, a sky full of shiny silver wings in V formation flying in from the South China Sea. Strangely, none had the familiar U.S. star marking the sides.

Instead his eyes focused on the flaming red Nippon suns. The markings on those Japanese Sally bombers seemed to burn holes through the sky.

Fran listened briefly to the hypnotic engines, well tuned, until it became clear the bomb bay doors under the painted red suns were open wide.

There was no advance warning, no declaration of war, just the sound of men screaming and engines bearing down. Fran hadn't heard about Pearl Harbor, Hawaii, didn't know it too had been attacked thousands of miles away across the Pacific Ocean and the International Dateline.

But now an explosion ripped—then another, then too many to count—up the runway, and he dashed for the mango trees circling the airstrip, shielding himself from the flying debris and the yellow flames that began baking those beautiful American aircraft into twisted black skeletons. The heat followed him in waves, as if it knew beforehand where he was running and meant to swallow him whole. He couldn't believe it was happening. Not now, not with all those planes lined up defenseless on the runway.

The timing of the Nippon attack was perfect and the proud Army airplane mechanics who meticulously kept their machines running watched them smolder on the runway, black smoke from their rubber tires smudging the blue sky. After the bombers came the Zeroes, flying low enough that you could see the shadowy pilots inside, machine gunning anything that moved. See me, see me, see me, their bullets screamed.

A handsome young man with shocking blonde hair flopped uncontrollably in the tall grass near a burning hangar, his severed leg a butcher shop bone. Another stared numbly at the bloody hamburger that was his arm. Shock. Anger. Gasoline trucks near the hangars were the first to explode, and beneath their charry remains lay the bodies of men who'd mistakenly sought protection there. So many mistakes, so much to learn about war, real war, not just boot camp training. Blindness, decapitation, mutilation, the manuals prepared no one for this and the smell of burning airplanes and the mournful whipsaw of bodies scissored apart by flying debris. All in less than an hour. It was amazing how quickly lives turned—one story told, another thrust upon them. The smug recruiter in that Wenatchee post office said nothing about this part of soldiering.

Defeat hung over the burning outpost. Clark Field's machine shops and hangars that'd been carefully carved out of the wild jungle now smoldered, and the runway was bomb blasted into craters the size of small lakes. Fifty-five Americans dead. The Japanese lost only two planes and just like at Pearl Harbor, to the world's eyes, the Americans seemed unprepared and unready to fight. Perhaps, as the Japanese so brazenly gambled, this war in the Pacific was over before it started.

The next hours passed in raw confusion and Fran spent the war's first night separated from his squadron, shivering in the open and listening to lonesome jungle sounds drifting from the thick black cover of bamboo and stringy vines that seemed to grab for him. It was the blackest night in his life. Smooth giant hardwoods, twelve feet around, stretched high into the air with limbs spread like umbrellas at the top. Even during the day, underneath those trees loomed a gloomy semi-darkness. Snakes and rats slithered over and around, climbing bamboos, tree ferns, mosses, orchids, and dry Nipa fronds. The sounds seemed to rush at him, play with him, laugh at his fear. In time he would grow used to the sounds of the jungle, but not that first night.

The Clark Field bombing was a warm-up for the arrival of Japanese General Masaharu Homma and the fire-breathing artillery of his 14th Army.

It wasn't long before the dragons positioned their big artillery pieces throughout Luzon and merciless ground attacks began. Manila was evacuated, triggering a rapid retreat into the Bataan Peninsula where the cutoff American and Filipino troops prepared for a showdown among the bamboo fields, ravines, and wooded mountains.

The Japanese were in a sweat to finish off Bataan, so they could aim their huge artillery at Corregidor, the small defiant island fortress that sat just two miles from Bataan and blocked the shipping lanes in and out of Manila Bay. Out on that rocky island, Marine Private Jack Elkins and Army Sergeant Odas Greer waited their turn. Greer, who grew up not far from Everett, Washington, already had been in the Army a few years and commanded two machine gun nests near the Corregidor beachfront. He and Jack, who crouched in a nearby foxhole, listened to the Japanese artillery rumbling across the water, punishing the Allied troops on Bataan. Not far away on the tiny island, Galen Martin split duty as an Army mess sergeant and height finder on an anti-aircraft gun latched tight to Morrison Hill. He felt young and exposed, and had a growing sense that his fate, like those on Bataan, soon would be settled.

The final push for Bataan began on Good Friday, April 3, 1942, when 50,000 Japanese soldiers, backed by 150 heavy artillery pieces, attacked Mt. Samat, Bataan's last line of defense. Big Japanese Sallys dropped incendiary bombs that licked the treetops and roasted everyone in their path below. The vicious assault continued for a week.

Ammo dumps exploded, brilliant fiery shows in the jungle night. There was confusion everywhere, with lost men tramping crowded, dark roads, shouting the names of friends. They were tired, sick, hungry, and defeated.

Their voices evaporated in the noisy confusion of dust-coated trucks, tanks, and wave after wave of injured men. Other wounded lay in ditches, waiting to die. Japanese planes strafed the road and artillery shells whooshed through bamboo thickets.

The day that the Americans surrendered, Fran stood in a field cleared of its fronds and vines, nursing an emptiness he couldn't imagine was possible.

Then he heard them coming from out of the distance, Japanese tanks screeching down the narrow road leading to where the Flying Infantry bivouacked. Before long the Japanese were upon them, some small, others surprisingly tall—intense, impatient men with gleaming bayonets.

Three arm-bound Americans under guard during the Bataan Death March; note captive Filipino soldiers in the background. *National Archives*

The American flag in the rough little jungle clearing was lowered and one of the Japanese soldiers kicked it. Another spat. Fran checked his anger. They, all of them, had surrendered, letting America down.

"You fightin' days over," someone growled in singsong English.

Now he felt the future coming at him, rising from the jungle heat like a biblical storm.

Keep walking, Fran told himself, as another halting bootprint was etched into the dust. Keep walking.

Soon the outline of one prisoner, another, and another joined together in one unbroken procession as far as his eyes could see down the cruel foreign road through the sun-drenched cane.

Each step was a mantra; it alone made sense of his army's surrender.

To stumble now, unless friendly hands reached for you and pushed you forward, brought death quick and sure. No court existed to hear your pleas.

The march to Camp O'Donnell took a couple days for some prisoners, more than a week for others, depending where on Bataan they surrendered. They quickly shed blankets, spare clothes, and shoes, for even the smallest weight became an unbearable burden in the tropical sun.

The rest the Japanese took for souvenirs: rings, watches, and eyeglasses, shaking down their captured chattel as if they were common criminals— worse than criminals, worse even than beasts. On the Bataan Death March generals walked alongside enlisted men, for animals had no rank.

Those with lips chapped with thirst covered their heads with broad green Nipa leaves, deflecting the sun's vertical rays that bore witness to the one absolute passed unspoken through the columns of weakened prisoners walking three- or four-wide on the oven-like road: "If you have a friend beside you and the friend falls, consider him dead, 'cause if you stop to pick him up or help him out you're gone too, by bayonet or by bullet."

Soon the march was a hallucination; voices reached out to coax you down. If you stopped to listen you might feel the words, soft as dead breezes on a hot summer day. It was your name they were speaking, it was your life they wanted. If you stumbled you were gone.

Carrying the wounded and disabled, Bataan Death March, April 1942. *National Archives*

There were no answers for such hauntings and so Fran simply recorded them as a movie camera might, one step taken, another left behind, walking bones and gristle.

The column swept him up and carried him down a road past palm and banana trees, through bamboo thickets and coconut forests that grew together at odd angles and seemed to add to the disorder. They crossed the scorching mudflats of the Candaba Swamp where tall reed-like grasses and lotus plants became mirages in the shimmering heat. One step, then another.

The Japanese badly underestimated the number of their Filipino and American prisoners and were unprepared, indifferent, and worse, unwilling to share their food and medicine with the 76,000 they herded down the narrow road to prison camp. Instead of an honorable death in battle, the tall pale Americans had surrendered. They were weak and unworthy, an inferior race.

Fran followed the blurry backs stretching far into the distance, a scraggly living column of hide and bone coursing through the endless brown-green countryside.

Alongside the road dark-skinned Filipino natives left cans holding delicious, beautiful clean water. They ached for it, as nothing before. More than once the guards kicked over the cans, and the prisoners, their tongues turning to stone, watched the precious liquid evaporate. Water to mud and then to dust.

Fran wore a ragged shirt with rolled-up sleeves and cutoff pants. Strapped to his Army web belt was a metal canteen cup on one hip, mess kit on the other. The cup rose up and down, up and down, with each step, a steady rhythm that reminded him of his unquenched thirst.

In that way he passed sinkholes of swamp-green water. Lying in those rancid wallows were bloated carabao floating on their sides, and the sweet odor of death drifted across the road. Clouds of black flies buzzed over them. There were other bodies as well, lying face down in the wallows: American soldiers who had survived months of hunger and jungle rot only to cash it in on a mad dash for a mouthful of infested water.

When a thirst-crazed prisoner broke ranks and bolted for the wallows, unruffled guards drew down and shot. Target practice. Another body added to the miserable puddle. Yet the rancid water smelled delicious. You had to fight the animal urge within you to join them.

There was no leadership, no command, no law. So he kept moving, picking his way forward on shaky legs and blistered feet, waiting always for the crack of a rifle or the rip of a knife. Living became minute to minute and without rules, a prehistoric reflex shaped by defeat.

The journey was strewn with corpses. Images in the distance drew into focus: It was an officer tied to a wood post in the blistering sun, his naked back a purple roadmap of horsewhipped welts, flies feeding at the open wounds. It was a sallow faced prisoner on his knees awaiting decapitation, a glinting Samurai sword poised above him.

Keep moving, don't stop, don't look.

Finally, he came upon a bruised American prisoner digging a grave—his own grave—in the sunshine not far off the road.

The column was ordered to stop. Perhaps the prisoner tried to escape, more likely he unknowingly insulted a guard—maybe the guard was just in a disagreeable mood. Because of it, someone had to die and someone had to watch. The prisoner bent to his shovel, an air of numb detachment to his labor. When he finished he was ordered to lie down in the grave, his eyes open and staring. With a shake of his rifle the guard motioned other prisoners to begin shoveling. Disobey and they would join him.

First the skinny legs and belly disappeared under shovelfuls of plain brown earth. Eventually then his face, with puffs of air snorting from around his mouth until it too disappeared, under shoveful after shoveful. Buried alive. Before long the mound of fresh turned dirt was just another grave, just another marker pointing the way.

It was commonplace for people to be shot and stabbed on the march. You get hard to it, you can't do nothing about it, so you keep going and say "I hope it's not me." That's the size of it. It's basic. It seems cruel but what else is there?—Fran Agnes

This wasn't settling a battlefield score; this was personal, criminal, hateful. It crept through the guards like a virus, gathering mob strength until the prisoners were swept along by its power and everything about the march blurred in a violent red mist.

By day four Fran had walked 60 miles to reach Camp O'Donnell, an old Filipino Army training post built to hold 500, now stuffed with 20,000 and growing.

When he pulled up inside its barbed wire fences under the unrelenting heat of the Filipino countryside, a squat, bald Japanese commander waited atop a wood box. This too would become familiar.

The camp's interpreter stood alongside with a bullhorn, reforming the venomous Japanese words into something recognizable in the hot afternoon air. A helluva show, all in all. The prisoners listened for a while and then lost interest. Their eyes could see that here one nightmare traded on the back of another.

Clouds of flies swarmed over the open trench latrines where men, dying of dysentery, squatted in the stink of their own watery shit. You could taste the smell in your mouth.

Thousands of thirsty prisoners waited in line with canteens for a minute at one of three small water spigots that sputtered in frustrating fits. Others, wasted and feverish, lined up in the sun for a mess kit cup of Filipino lugaw, a thin rice soup. With luck, swimming inside might be a tablespoon of camote, the native sweet potato. Most times, the camote was a rotten chunk of bitter black bile.

Fran's eyes stopped at where the dead were piled, survivors of the death march who couldn't outlive Camp O'Donnell. Mass open graves had been dug and the nearly weightless bodies, some with dog tags clamped between their teeth, were tossed in one atop another, their bony arms and legs locked in death's embrace. Every so often one of the prisoners holding the pole of a burial litter collapsed from disease or starvation or maybe just resignation, and he too was tossed in the pile.

In less than three months, more than 20,000 Filipinos and 1,400 Americans died inside O'Donnell. One day alone, 548 Filipinos and Americans succumbed—roughly one every three minutes.

"You no longer belong to America," the agitated Japanese commander screamed at another batch of arrivals, forced to stand for hours at attention without cover under the tropical sun. "You are the property of the Imperial Emperor of Japan, the Son of Heaven. From now on you will bow to all Japanese soldiers from generals to privates. Their word is your word. To disobey is to die."

And to die, they could see, wasn't a particularly long journey, Fran knew. It sank in for all the others too. O'Donnell was just the beginning. Those who survived graduated to Camp Cabanatuan, 100 miles north of Manila, where prison life would sort itself out on a scale closely approximating hell.

3

All the rules were crumbling

LOW MILK CLOUDS SKITTERED across the anxious tropical sky, smudging the moon until every shadow seemed darker, every footstep sinister. All hands, from the unfed Marines waiting in dirty foxholes, to the officers and nurses in the great concrete Malinta Tunnel, knew the score.

Wave after wave of Japanese soldiers, like thousands of beady spiders, soon would swarm over the white sand and rock beaches and steadily up the scrubby bluff where judgement waited. Such sureness made every heart pump faster. There was nothing else; forgotten even was the terrible doubt that followed weeks of isolation and dwindling rations. Night after night, dusk had ground down into darkness, sweaty and joyless over the island of Corregidor.

Anticipating invasion, a searchlight swept the broken shoreline, the beam from its unblinking yellow eye swallowed up in the black void that was Manila Bay. Eventually an enemy marksman from across the water shot it out with a brilliant explosion of sizzling sparks. Full night returned, with only the sound of waves slapping the beach.

In his Bataan headquarters, General Homma felt the stubbornness of the American and Filipino troops who hunkered in and took his wrath day after lousy day. First they had clawed into the jungles of Bataan and had to be starved out. Now the island fortress of Corregidor across the water to the south resisted him as well. The Japanese general, who had engineered the American-Filipino surrender in Bataan a few weeks earlier and oversaw the death march to Camp O'Donnell, turned his mobile artillery toward Corregidor with its huge protected mortars, tunnels, and dug-in defenders.

Jack Elkins, U.S. Marine Corps.

Corregidor blocked the entrance to Manila Bay and he needed the way cleared if the Japanese were to control the Philippines and conquer the Pacific.

So for weeks, General Homma filled the two miles of sky between Bataan and Corregidor with 400 pound artillery shells; each one, it sometimes seemed, with an obituary tagged to it. Rocks on the island burst apart in showering splinters of flashing green light. Patches of jungle, once alive with hibiscus and orchids, wilted under the burning shells.

One unforgettable day, the Japanese unleashed 240 mm shells every five seconds for five straight hours, their unrelenting concussions shuddering the spiny, limestone island until some Americans, crazy with fright, climbed from their foxholes and ran.

That was how you died, Marine Private Jack Elkins assured himself as he knelt deep in his foxhole fighting off the urge to run. The scorched island that resembled a long, thin tadpole from the air was only 3½ miles long and 1½ miles at its widest. They wouldn't let him in the Malinta Tunnel, not beach fodder like him. No, it was safer anyway, ducked down in a dugout hole away from the whining artillery that gave three or four seconds warning before murdering everything in its path.

Jack had placed two-foot-high canisters filled with sand around the rim of his foxhole. A bamboo pole covered with green fronds camouflaged the homemade shanty; the barrel of his Springfield rifle scanned across the porcupine grasses and low creepers to the rocky beach below where the invaders would land. Later, he would discover, it was a perfect place for killing.

For weeks he expected to die, had accepted it, really. He saw no other way off Corregidor and was surprised he'd lasted this long. A piece of kindling, that's all he was in the great fire around him.

He reached for the yellow-striped lard can at his feet and swallowed a gulp of tepid, silty water. It soothed his dusty throat. He returned the can to its place alongside the boxes of hand grenades. The yellow-striped can reminded him of a barber pole and barber poles reminded him of home. The minutes quietly evaporated.

Nearby, Army Sergeant Odas Greer and the men of Battery M, 60th Coast Artillery, also waited, their machine guns tethered into two anti-aircraft gun pits pointing beachward.

Empty ammunition boxes made of wood with metal sides were stacked atop one another, so that enemy bullets would hit the boxes and not the rock walls and ricochet into the pit where Greer and his men passed the night.

A slight breeze tried pushing the white clouds away, but mostly the night air was heavy and sluggish. From his position, Greer could stand and see across South Shore Road, the Kindley Field landing strip, and skinny North Shore Road running along the bluff. The beach, dark and lonely, was less than a thousand yards away and that was where the Japs would come. It was as if he smelled them already.

Greer ducked down between the anti-aircraft machine guns, watching his soldiers hidden in the pit, nervously smoking cigarettes.

Newman, the Jewish kid from New York, had diarrhea, and every so often he'd apologetically shit into an empty ammunition box and dump it over the side. At least for now, the thick cigarette cloud masked the foul odor and discouraged the nagging black flies.

Beside him was another pit also with .50 and .30 caliber machine guns. Six men to a pit—Hackett, Newlick, Riley, Roberts, Rudder, Cook, Steuss, Stuts, Sawyer, Newsome, Newman, Poke, good men all. Greer knew every one of them. Before 24 hours were up, five would be dead. Maybe they were the lucky ones.

Greer's men occupied the last two machine gun pits on the far east end of the island, near the grassy overgrown cemetery that was parched free of trees. Just beyond them sat Hooker Point, the rocky tail of the tadpole. Across the bay northeast stood Manila.

Greer, who at 28 was older than most of the men, blew reveille in the morning and taps at night. He was short, wiry, athletic, and sometimes called The Bugler, although not particularly to his face. He was jumpy this night like the others, too, but there was an air of confidence about him. He'd eaten Army chow for several years already and had no intention of dying on this bombed-out place they called The Rock.

Greer's view across the dark burned-off expanse was much different now than when he arrived before the war and saw Corregidor's palm trees clutch lazily in the soft breeze. There also had been mango and cashew trees and blooming orchids. There were big glasses of beer for a dime at the canteen and trolley trains, so when you were on Bottomside by the entrance to the Malinta Tunnel you could catch a ride to Middleside. Honest to God, just like San Francisco.

On Topside, near the squat gun batteries of the island's 59th and 60th Coast Artillery, sat a thick barracks building. There also was a PX, chapel, parade grounds, and nine-hole golf course.

On clear nights, homesick soldiers watched the starry headlights on Dewey Boulevard in Manila some distance away, twinkling seductively as if it were the Golden Gate Bridge across the water.

Boot camp—148th Platoon, U.S. Marine Corps, San Diego, December 1940. Included in this group of trainees were Jack Elkins, Jerry Hanson, and Roy A. Wederbrook.

It was only a ferry ride over to those dusky sweet women of Manila. Singing street vendors strolled past open-fronted bars and the heavy smell of fried foods clung to the streets. A night at the Manila Hotel cost a dollar. For three dollars, a soldier bought quite a weekend, riding the horse-drawn calesa carts and chasing those smart city gals. The native gin burned your nostrils and teared your eyes. The days were warm and slow moving, the nights just easy.

Even on Corregidor it was swell, they had written in letters home. In the evening after a day of training, topsiders would grab the trolley or hustle down 180 stairs to the canteen's beer garden on Middleside. They'd stand together in the pleasant tropical breeze and let the friendly banter wash over them. For children of America's Great Depression, Army life wasn't at all bad. They believed in thrift and hard work and that their defense of the Philippines would somehow save the Pacific. Protecting was a coat that fit them well.

Although every sign clearly pointed to it, many of them still didn't believe the Japanese would actually touch off a war and ruin everything. But that's exactly what happened.

The proof came just hours after Pearl Harbor when the wave of Japanese planes surprised Clark Field near Manila with a raid so methodical in its execution and destruction that it took less than an hour. Next, invading Japanese troops turned their guns on the American infantry and support troops who fled into the jungles of Bataan. It was an ugly, protracted fight that slowly choked off the Americans and Filipinos. When Bataan surrendered, Corregidor, with its nearly 16,000 American and Filipino troops, knew what was next.

Greer ducked low day after day, as strips of jungle around him were artilleried into stumps and the infantry driven into foxholes. Shelling flattened the topside barracks and golf course, and anyone without the good sense to duck. Wildfires spread unchecked and thick smoke roiled over the island. What had been green jungle was barraged into an ugly ash-black. If anyone had been crazy enough to try, they could practically play baseball in the open, stubby fields.

A few hundred yards east of Greer and his machine guns, Jack Elkins squatted alone in his pear-shaped foxhole dug into the rocky soil of Corregidor's farthest outcropping. The very tip of the tadpole's tail. Jack was the youngest in his squad and assigned the tail's farthest flank facing Bataan, with the whole island to his left and lonely Manila Bay his sole companion on the right.

Most mornings, an ominous, sausage-shaped observation balloon rose beyond the massive Japanese artillery positions hidden in Bataan's wooded hills. The balloon warned the Americans of the shelling about to begin. Peeping Tom they called the dark, tethered balloon and every day it told Jack to snuggle deep into his foxhole.

Jack sometimes thought of the American officers, along with the female nurses, safe in bomb-proof Malinta Tunnel. When the shooting began weeks earlier, the officers had hustled their cots inside, where they were safe as school kids under the blue mercury vapor lights.

The main tunnel was 30 feet wide and a quarter mile long, blasted out of rock decades earlier and coated with strong reinforced concrete. It was stuffy inside and so dusty you could almost see the air itself hanging around the generators, hospital cots, and stores of canned food and water.

The rumor in the foxholes was that some officers had tunnelitis so bad they were afraid to come out even to shit. They probably had plenty to eat, too, while the beach defenders ate their watery tomato sauce slopped over rice. Steak and potatoes. Apple pie and ice cream. It wasn't hard to let your mind wander.

Near Jack on the bluff overlooking the water was Roy A. Wederbrook of Hereford, Texas. A few days earlier, Jack watched as Wederbrook dug his machine gun pit about halfway down the rocky slope facing Bataan.

"Ain't backin' up no further," Wederbrook drawled when Jack pointed out that the Texan had planted himself in direct line of the invasion. If it came to that, he'd die dug into the bluff, he told Jack. A helluva place to cash it in and a long way from the Texas Panhandle.

Within Jack's reach in his foxhole was a Browning Automatic Rifle, commonly called a BAR, a Springfield 30.06, four cases of hand grenades, stacks of ammunition, and that old lard can of water. Home sweet home.

Jack's eyes drifted over the still nighttime beach and for a moment simply watched the phosphorescence in Manila Bay, a pretty blue-green that shone like an undersea lantern. For all its terror, Corregidor was not complicated, you honored its formalities or you died.

And so late every evening when the shelling from Bataan eased up, Jack mechanically searched out the chow truck hidden in the shadow of scrub vines and burned-out branches on South Shore Road. If you wanted dinner, tomato sauce over rice, your nose found the truck.

On this night he maneuvered away from his foxhole to where he imagined the chow truck would be. A breeze finally pushed away the clouds and night broke free making the island, otherwise lost, the center target in the Pacific War.

A strange sound seemed to drift in off the bay. He stopped and listened. What was that? He strained forward, moving towards the bluff's edge. He thought he heard engines grinding out in the water. He studied the waves. The phosphorescence stirred. Then he saw them.

For a heartbeat he was too stunned to move. Then he bolted back across the grassy bluff to his foxhole and jumped in, his heart racing. Finally, after weeks of shelling from Japanese guns and bombardments from their planes, the invasion was here. It would end now one way or another. Man against man, flesh against flesh. Like Wederbrook had said, there was no retreat. At age 19, Jack's world had come to this.

He pulled himself out of the foxhole and crouched nearby, his Browning Automatic Rifle and a pile of ammo magazines at his side. A staccato of gunfire erupted along the beach, and bullets popped like rivets when striking the metal-plated landing boats. He sought a deep breath, aimed into the darkness, and squeezed the trigger. God help us all.

The Japanese landing boats floated 75 yards out and about all he could make of the beach was the phosphorous foam kicking up and the Japanese 61st Infantry running through it. Machine gun fire rang in his ears and there was nothing else, no other sounds, no other thoughts. Alone, a soldier at last.

From the beach somewhere, a powerful searchlight suddenly swept the bay. Frozen in its baleful yellow stare were three blunt-end landing barges with young Japanese soldiers spilling out into waist deep surf. Dozens of the enemy with long rifles already clogged Corregidor's shore, and they huffed blindly up the craggy beach to escape the curtain of bullets that pinged down and ricocheted into the sea. Within seconds, the searchlight exploded in fissures of sparkling light and the burning image of Japanese soldiers running for their lives slowly evaporated.

More than a mile to Jack's left, American troops poured from the Malinta Tunnel, hoping to rebuff the invasion's thrust. The tide had swept the first of General Homma's landing boats off course, towards the tail of the tadpole where Jack waited; his automatic rifle already hot with wild shots into the night. Droplets of gun oil speckled his face.

Out in the bay a boat exploded and incandescent flames crackled up and out of it. For a few moments it stole Jack's attention. It was an eerie vision, as if he were peering through a spider's web; the light on the other side splintered and diffused a thousand ways. The fire backlit the Japanese soldiers running on the rocky beach faster and faster, until they were beyond the flame's bright glow and night swallowed them whole.

There was a moment when he saw them run past the licking flames and then nothing. Rub your eyes and they were gone. Maybe they never existed. The vision seared into him and left him wondering if what he saw in the fiery reflection off the water was real, or something else, perhaps the silvery negative from a picture.

They were strange creatures, these Japanese soldiers now suddenly within rifle range. Some wore wrapped khaki puttees and webbed helmets, disciples of the ancient Japanese Samurai code. They didn't surrender. They would run and run and run out of the boats, out of the water, until the island was theirs.

Near him came the steady hacking of Wederbrook's machine gun. He listened for its familiar voice, which comforted him in a way, as would the melody of a mournful song.

Jack loaded a magazine of tracer bullets into his BAR, aimed, and blasted away into the front of a landing craft. Too late he realized the tracers were simply a lighted path right back to him. *Stupid,* he thought, and hit the ground as bullets nicked around him, phht, phht, phht off the sullen earth. *They are shooting at me.* It was several minutes before it was quiet. He crabbed back to his foxhole and dove in.

Jack had been in combat about 15 minutes, but already time seemed irrelevant—15 minutes could've been 15 hours for all it mattered.

A sergeant from D Company, holding a .45 caliber pistol in one hand, slipped down the trail behind Jack's foxhole, his breath escaping in ragged gasps. The sergeant had been checking his machine gun nests when he found himself in the island's old cemetery. It was dark and ghostly as all graveyards at night. He nearly bumped into a Japanese soldier and almost jumped out of his skin.

"Nip tried to bayonet me so I shot him," the sergeant whispered to Jack. He carried the pistol in his hand, as if holstering the piece would make the dead Japanese rise again and come at him from the grave.

The sergeant rested in Jack's foxhole a minute or two until his breathing steadied. Then he disappeared.

When Jack looked out, the vessel still burned in the water, kicking out smoky illusions. Although the majority of boats landed far to his left at North Point, more than 700 Imperial soldiers hit the beach before him.

It was then Jack remembered the leftover World War I bombs he'd stockpiled several days earlier. He and another Marine had rigged together several crude wooden chutes, so the bombs could slide down and explode when striking the beach below.

As the sounds of gunfire continued, Jack crept along a narrow path worn into the porcupine grass until he came to the first stack of bombs. The enemy had to be positioned directly underneath the wooden chutes for the makeshift system to work. Strange voices drifted up from various huddles on the beach, but they were nowhere near the chute bottoms. The plan would be useless unless he could think of something fast.

As quietly as possible, Jack lifted one of the bombs and inched himself around the dark, still bushes, until he stood over the voices. He had quarterbacked his Oakesdale, Washington, high school football team. Now, not many months removed from those farm-town Friday night games, he was a quarterback again. He cocked and delivered. The 35 pound bomb tumbled awkwardly off his hand end over end, crashing into the darkness below. Thud. Nothing. He lay on the bluff for a moment, waiting. Then he silently crept away to where he'd hidden another stack. This time he spiraled one over the edge underhand. The explosion shook him for a second. Then it was quiet on the beach. He repeated the underhand toss at another location nearby and again it stilled the voices below.

So the night passed. The piles of dead were left behind like sacks of garbage on the shoreline or partway up the bluff where they had fought towards the island's big mortars.

Sometime before dawn, Jack retreated to his foxhole and snuggled down inside, exhausted. He closed his eyes.

"You can fight your damn war," he murmured to no one, for he was quite alone. In seconds he was asleep.

Sergeant Greer ordered the machine guns to the rim of the anti-aircraft pit the instant that the landing boats broke the surf below him. Red tracers arced over North Shore Road and the beachline, plinking against the boats' protective metal plates before careening off into the bay. Occasionally his guns swept the beach, unknowing of the damage they rent in the dark. A bitter, burnt, cordite smell clung about the concrete pit.

Up top Greer was vulnerable to the return fire of the Japanese, but at least the shooting angles were better. Besides, he wasn't one for backing down.

In combat, Greer soon discovered there are blank stretches of silence wedged between flurries of shooting. Silence then shooting. There was a rhythm to it, like blowing a bugle. For a while it was no more complicated than a sergeant giving orders and his men following through. Such strangeness filled the dark spaces of Corregidor that night.

Then, as the first pink streaks of dawn traced the Philippine sky, word came that the Japanese had cut the island in two and reinforcements were needed near Malinta Hill with its labyrinth of bombproof tunnels.

Greer ordered his men to toss the firing bolts from the two .50 caliber machine guns into the deep bay. The rules had changed. Now he needed speed and mobility and the big guns were too heavy to be lugged about by hand. Only neutered weapons would be left behind.

In his mind Greer knew the battle for the Philippines had been lost months earlier when the allied leaders agreed to stop Hitler in Europe first, leaving the forces on Bataan and Corregidor to fight the Japanese army alone. Without reinforcements, and as food and ammunition ran dangerously low, even a stalemate was impossible. They'd bluffed as long as they could. In a way, they could almost count it as a victory, holding out so long. But he suspected that no one back home would see it that way or understand the complexities.

After the oily bolts disappeared into the dull water, morning seemed to break free of its nighttime moorings. Darkness was a hindrance, but it also had provided protection.

Greer stopped for a moment and watched the vivid tropical morning deliver itself. But when his eyes left the sky and sea and drifted landward, the picture was stained by veins of Japanese soldiers coursing further and further inland from the beaches, their dusty boots trodding over terraced bluffs of black, scorched soil. Snapped onto their Arisaka rifles were sharp bayonets—so altogether, man and weapon, they appeared quite menacing.

"Move," Greer barked and the men from the machine gun nests slipped warily away towards Water Tank Hill in direct collision with the invaders.

At last now he would see the enemy up close in daylight and take their full measure. For the longest time on Corregidor, distance had blurred everything.

Suddenly, a Japanese soldier sprang from the lip of an artillery shell hole, his fist clutching a grenade. Strangely, it reminded Greer of a beer can, tumbling in slow motion through the clear morning air. Maybe this is how a batter sees a curveball, seams twisting with unmistakable clarity towards home plate. Ted Williams, Stan Musial, DiMaggio. There was barely time to curse it. There was only time for he and his men to curl around their .30 caliber machine gun and wait. On came the grenade, pulled by the gravity of its impersonal killing.

The explosion tossed Greer backwards and upwards, where he was fully exposed to the Japanese soldier who drew down his bayoneted rifle in one easy motion. The bullet pierced Greer's Army web belt, then his thick first aid packet, before breaking flesh and cutting toward his bladder. At first he was only aware of the grenade's shell fragments peppering his chest. Then a sharp kick in the stomach from the bullet. Then the terrible, roaring, all-consuming pain. He lay where he fell on the neutral soil, assessing all the ways his body might fail.

Time jerked by now like scenes in a homemade movie, movement without transition. Gunfire spat around him; he heard it and then not. He opened his eyes. The Jap disappeared, probably thought him dead. Maybe he was. Everyone else was gone too and the light in his brain faded into black. For some incalculable time it was like that. Then his head cleared long enough to see an American standing over him, the side of his face slick with blood where his ear had been sliced off, jagged and ugly, as if someone had attacked it with a dull knife. *Your ear is missin',* he thought, even as he lay there dying. *Your ear is missin', your ear is missin'. Shit.*

The bleeding soldier silently wrapped an arm around Greer's shoulders and muscled him over the rocks into a Navy communications tunnel where the sounds of war were muted and distant. A row of blurry electric bulbs in metal cones shone a weird, unnatural glow. It was unbearably stuffy and hot. Dust and fear made it hard to breathe. The soldier laid him on the concrete alongside a growing collection of badly wounded men. Blood smeared Greer's uniform into a damp, sticky red and an overworked medic soon appeared with scissors to cut it off around his belly and legs.

He was filled with metal nuggets and the bullet had nicked his bladder, but Greer's web belt and first aid packet saved him. Pain grew from a dull throb in the legs to a sharp gnaw in the stomach. Blood trickled out and scabbed dark and crusty in the humid air. The sound of groans, the stares from unfocused eyes. He would survive, but there was no telling what sort of life it'd be with the Japanese now in control of the island. They would deal with him soon enough.

During moments of peace on Corregidor, Greer thought of his mother back home in the damp Pacific Northwest not far from Everett. He was an only child who left home to join the Army in the 1930s and worked his way up to sergeant. No regrets. He gave orders and took orders. A good soldier, a good son. And yet what would his mother be doing now—maybe thinking of him? Perhaps gently gripping a fountain pen and composing her thoughts in a letter. Maybe he'd see her again someday, bent over in her backyard garden working the rich soil in a fine Northwest mist.

Jack raised his pocked metal helmet slowly until his eyes crossed the lip of the foxhole and he gazed onto the beach below. Thoughts of the night yet filled him. The sun would soon matter-of-factly evaporate the dew from the remaining hibiscus leaves, but not so his memories of the fight. It would be another clear, hot day on this island that seemed locked into itself in the blue water, buffeted by an incessant wind. His Marine khakis were streaked with dirt and dried sweat, and his fingers and arms were like the roots of trees grown from the craggy soil. His face was unshaven and rough, as if he'd aged overnight. Mostly, Jack was surprised to be alive.

Just offshore, the empty Japanese landing boats were clearly defined now, stark and real, though less threatening in the early morning light, their blunt metal ramps left open where hours earlier enemy soldiers filed ashore. Seawater lapped lazily inside the swamped, useless vessels. It was peaceful in a way, dissimilar in every measure to the night that had just passed. Maybe, he could have hoped, Corregidor would stay that way.

But even at first glance the island suggested disappointment.

Almost against his will, Jack's eyes peered out of his foxhole until resting upon four Japanese soldiers not 35 yards away. They were preparing breakfast between rocks on the white sand beach, quietly oblivious to anyone else, particularly an American Marine peering from the overhanging bluff. Under different conditions it might've been serene: four friends sharing a few moments together on a tropical island beachfront. Their rifles lay alongside them on the rocks, the breeze blowing past their faces.

Jack studied them. They appeared to be talking, but he was too removed on the bluff to catch even feathery snatches of their strange language. He was alone on his end of the island, the rest of B Company tucked behind on safer, less exposed terrain. There was no way of knowing how many were alive. The hammering from Wederbrook's machine gun long ago had been silenced, and if Jack had had the power to turn invisible and fly over the body-strewn beach he would've found his friend draped lifeless over the machine gun, his boots covered in spent bullet casings and his shirt removed in the heat of the fight. Jack knew and didn't need to see. He ran his tongue across his dry lips, deciding what to do.

The enemy foot soldiers on the beach before him, unassuming in their baggy summer uniforms, now ate breakfast, still conversing in hushed tones. Perhaps they'd grown up together somewhere in a prefecture in Japan. Maybe they'd worked in flooded rice paddies or studied in the same school. They had parents and possibly children of their own.

He suspected that once they finished their morning rations, however, their first project would be to sweep over this far end of the island and they wouldn't be forgiving, they wouldn't hesitate, they wouldn't be thinking of *his* parents.

Jack reached for the BAR and felt his fingers curl around its cool indifference. He brought it to his shoulder. He scoped down its long, straight barrel. It would be a clean, unhurried burst. No excuses now. He stilled his breathing and found the huddle of Japanese soldiers, one anonymous mass of green uniforms, web belts, and canteens, still eating, still oblivious to judgment calling from above. Soldiers don't hesitate, soldiers don't have to think.

Coarse, ugly shots shocked the morning calm. Finger to trigger, bullets to flesh. Two of the soldiers slumped over, cold food spilling from their surprised fingers. The other two stood and bolted crazily down the beach, their split-toed boots scuffling rocky sand. Jack followed them in his sights, a hunter smelling prey. It was all instinct now. When he shot they dropped as well and lay with all the others from the night before on the beach. That was it. Four dead from his hand alone.

Jack's eyes returned to the breakfast camp on the rocks, now littered with the two lives first taken. He watched the still, solemn bodies for a moment. A short while ago they were eating breakfast, talking, planning their day.

Maybe for a second as the sound reached their ears and the bullets struck their flesh, maybe for that second they knew they were dead.

He glanced back to the shoreline where the other two had scrambled, trying to escape when the shooting began. He immediately found one, a lifeless heap on the sand right where he had felled him. Jack's eyes searched for the other, the last one. He was gone, disappeared. He looked again. No, there was no mistake. There were three dead, not four. So, maybe they all were pretending, waiting for him to gaze elsewhere so they too could escape and then come back and kill him.

Jack pulled his single action Springfield 30.06 from alongside him in the foxhole. There'd be no more playing possum. There'd be no Jap soldiers sneaking back later to root him out with their long bayoneted rifles. He aimed at the carcasses on the beach. He hadn't seen their faces, took no note of their features, couldn't tell later if they were tall, short, scarred, or clean. Each shot rang out without judgement, crack, crack, like dry tree limbs snapping. When each bullet struck, the bodies jumped as if Jack had walked up and personally kicked each in the belly.

Jack hadn't asked for this. He didn't thirst for blood. Nothing in his life prepared him for it.

They would've done the same, they would've shot him. That's war and you either accord its selfish rules or it's you lying in the sun on the beach covered with flies. Except no one warns you about how you can never scrub that image from your brain.

An hour later, with the sun burning hot, the three bodies on the beach began to twitch—quick, spastic movements as if there was life yet inside them waiting to finish their cold breakfast.

Sometime later, Japanese soldiers one by one began wading back into the warm bay towards a landing barge scuttled not far offshore. It was a curious thing. There must be something on one of those barges they need, Jack thought. One unlucky Japanese soldier after another had been sent back and out in the water. Jack never learned what they were after.

They were easy targets, leaping from beachfront cover into the breaking surf only 30 yards out.

Jack picked them off with his Springfield rifle as easily as prairie rabbits back home. Afterwards their bleeding bodies gently rose and fell with the waves, violent red staining peaceful blue.

It happened over and over, maybe a dozen times, and still they kept coming, one at a time running into the surf—red blood on blue water. The mind and body, Jack discovered that morning on Corregidor, have much to offer and much to lose.

Corregidor surrenders, early May 1942. *National Archives*

One terrified Japanese soldier never did swim ashore during the invasion. He clung about all night and morning inside a half-sunken landing barge, only his moon shaped face poking out. Every so often, Jack, still up in the foxhole playing God under the hot afternoon sun, aimed near him and watched as he dove under when the bullet plunked nearby. Thirty seconds later he'd bob up again. Such a bizarre game.

At any time Jack could've ended it with one shot, but he didn't. He had no taste for cold-blooded killing.

It's still real vivid in my mind. There is a lot of blood from a human being and when it comes up on the water it's really red. You see this sort of thing. In my mind if I went back and stood where I was before I think that's what I'd see. It's not a nice sight. The people who you've shot are down there and they're twitching yet, an hour later.—Jack Elkins

General Douglas MacArthur had bailed out of Corregidor weeks earlier, leaving the Philippine command to General Jonathan "Skinny" Wainwright, a popular soldier born in the wheat land of Walla Walla, Washington, not far from Jack's hometown.

It fell on Wainwright's shoulders to cable President Franklin Roosevelt that it would be surrender for the Pacific forces, "With broken heart and head bowed in sadness but not in shame."

Marine Corps radio operator Robert Raymond, an acquaintance of Jack's, listened on the headset as Wainwright ordered a surrender. Just before noon on May 6, 1942, Corregidor was lost.

"I do not feel very good at all…mostly just numb," Raymond later wrote.

The tiny island fortress stocked with mortars, artillery, and nearly 16,000 American and Filipino troops had withstood a firestorm from hell. Every day for weeks, more than 100 Japanese artillery pieces had thundered down on them from Bataan. Relentless enemy bombers from nearby Clark Field flew sortie after sortie, leaving behind dugout craters the size of small gullies. Rations had been cut, then cut again, and yet, as if by sheer tenacity, they held off the Japanese. Only with the Philippines surrendered could the Japanese fulfill their dream of creating a Greater East Asia Co-Prosperity Sphere. In their minds the Pacific would fall—nation by nation, island by island—until the four corners of the Nippon tent stretched across the Eastern World. Maybe it would happen just that way.

A few days before the invasion, ammunition for the island's big anti-aircraft guns ran out. Even so, if their food stocks weren't nearly depleted, Jack was convinced, they could've held out a little longer and slowed the Japanese plans for the Pacific.

General Homma was unhappy, as were his war leaders in Tokyo who had expected quick success in the Philippines. They were unaccustomed to delays in their march for dominance in the Greater East Asia War, Dai Toa Senso. Now there would be vengeance.

Greer lay on the concrete floor, blood-crusty bandages wrapped around his legs and belly, when the first of them burst into the tunnel. He felt a cold bayonet tip on his throat.

"Presento, presento," they screamed. The wounded soldiers reached for their wallets, watches, eyeglasses, and rings—souvenirs now for the enemy. Greer found no pity in their young faces.

Jack learned of the surrender later that afternoon out in his foxhole where, to his amazement, he was still alive. At any time during the day he expected a Japanese patrol to root him out. Once, when certain he heard them coming, he ducked deep into the shadows of the foxhole and pulled the pin on a grenade. If they came peeking inside, he'd pop up, hand it out, and they would all die together. But it never happened. Another strange twist of war.

Sometime during the overnight battle, he'd picked up a shell fragment in his leg, a slight, nicking wound. Like Wederbrook, he'd expected to die in the invasion, was prepared to do so, and had every reason to believe that's how his obituary would read in the Oakesdale newspaper. Front page maybe. "Local Marine Dies in Philippines" or something like that.

He unwrapped a Ration B chocolate bar he'd been saving and hungrily stuffed it in his mouth. He washed it down with the last of the warm water in the old striped lard can.

Before long, two Japanese soldiers in dirt-smudged uniforms appeared over the grassy bluff. All three sat together for a minute outside his foxhole smoking cigarettes, respectful of the battle just fought.

Afterwards with hand signals and brusque one-syllable grunts that were to become so familiar, Jack was ordered to march away with his Springfield rifle over his shoulder, bolt open and down.

Evening shadows fell through the cemetery when he joined the other captured American and Filipino soldiers from the end of the island, all kneeling silently in the dusty, shell-pocked cemetery road.

A few yards away, their animated captors argued, occasionally glancing at their hushed prisoners. Would they kill them quick here in the darkening cemetery or slowly later as war prisoners? The heated words flew back and forth as if they were debating the slaughter of farm animals.

Wind blew past him from the open bay. There was nothing left in the world to block it. Jack discovered to his amazement that he was first in line, closest to the Japanese. *There's something for you,* he thought. *First in line.* He'd made it a point as early as Marine boot camp to never volunteer or lead any line. The middle, that's where it's safest. Last foxhole on the island, first in the line of surrender. All the rules he'd established for himself were crumbling. But he'd already made up his mind. If the decision over there was to execute prisoners, Jack Orin Elkins was not going down meekly. He'd tackle the first Nip soldier he saw and make a break for it beyond the cemetery, where the evening tide was again quietly swallowing the rocks on Corregidor's stony beaches.

It would be a suicide run, but a bullet in the back trying sure as hell beats one in the head kneeling.

4

Our old world is crumbling
(Everett, 1942)

A HARD, HOMETOWN RAIN dripped into sidewalk puddles outside the old hotel where Ed Fox waited.

Even at this sleepy hour, the air was poisoned by a sour pulp mill smell that drifted back from the harbor under a closed-in sky. On such a Northwest night, the locals would say, anything might happen.

Wartime Everett, Washington, was similar in some ways to hometowns all over America and different in a lot of other ways that mattered. America's homefront was a lost cause for Jack, Odas, Fran, and the other captives overseas. It was a destination for letters that never arrived and memories that eventually turned against them.

But homefront Everett, with its smokestack waterfront and hard luck drinkers downtown, had war stories of its own. It was here Jack and Fran and some of the others would eventually settle, drawn in for different reasons. It was a city that even in 1942 held people like Ed Fox so tight they couldn't leave; it was a city in a time like no other.

Fox stared through the streaky windows of the Strand Hotel night after night, watching lonely soldiers cutting across Colby Avenue. He was the night clerk here, the check-in king of the hotel's rootless crowd: soldier, sailor, drunkard, whore.

By Fox's own admission it wasn't much of a kingdom. Even camouflaged by night and the Army's strict dim-out orders, the Strand was a remarkably depressing boxed building, with faded red brick stacked up and around chipped wood framed windows holding curtains that were rarely parted. Neglect and rain had worn down the hotel built 26 years earlier in the blast

Ed Fox, sitting comfortably amongst his collection of hardbounds. *Everett Public Library*

furnace of the last great war. But even in its sorry condition, the Strand didn't tell secrets.

Doors slammed upstairs. Couples, their eyes shiny with desire, pretended to be man and wife. Others collapsed in giggles at the thought. Tall and bookish, Fox saw it all and remembered most of it.

Unbeknownst to just about everyone, he possessed one of the finest minds in Everett. Had he been so inclined, he could've written a compelling treatise on the history of printing, or the origins of jazz. Instead he composed letters; great sprawling reports that flung open the curtains of a hotel most Everett residents would never deign to enter. They just knew the Strand was there is all, a dirty little refuge for the misfits in town. Strangely, Fox found refuge there as well.

"An odd lot of characters turn up in hotels—dubious looking men accompanied by still more dubious looking females, gents on a toot, gals on a toot, and the usual chorus of just plain stews," Fox wrote.

When he wasn't ruling over the check-in desk, Fox was at home several tree-lined blocks north on Wetmore Avenue. There, surrounded by stacks of books, he pecked away at his Oliver No. 9 typewriter, doodling on short stories or carrying forth with Russel Morehouse, a longtime friend who lived with his wife about 12 miles down Puget Sound in the waterfront village of Edmonds. Letters were their favored form of communication.

Fox wrote about the progress of the war, politics, authors, and, curiously more and more, about Gracie Emmett, a generally unremarkable woman who had moved into the Strand's room 38. The only thing graceful about Gracie was her legs, small and shapely, that pumped like pistons when she hurried off to her barmaid job downtown.

Despite his intellect, Fox never had strayed far from Everett, an unpretentious city that had grown out of the thick green landscape between Port Gardner Bay and the Snohomish River—hewn from ancient Douglas firs and Western red cedars so majestic even John D. Rockefeller once took notice.

There was profit to be made here if a businessman was shrewd enough and tough enough to bust the trees and the men needed to do it cheap. Everett grew up all right, and Rockefeller would've been impressed by its smokestack-belching waterfront, the busy commerce transacted downtown, and the hard working folks in their cherry tree neighborhoods that spiderwebbed back from the Rucker Hill mansions.

Downtown Everett and the Strand absorbed Fox, regardless of his bow ties and scholarly demeanor. He found a crazy rhythm to his liking among the hotel's dim lights, the ashtray stands, and the musty, overstuffed davenport that was often occupied by a late-night soldier or downtown floozy hoping to pass the night.

Aside from cheap owners who cut the lobby's heat after midnight and the battle axe who worked the swing shift (and jumped him the second he entered the place with a full report of trouble brewing in the rooms upstairs), life was turning out okay in wartime Everett.

And then Gracie landed at the Strand one day and for a while everything got a little better.

When Gracie arrived she let everyone know, loudly of course, that it wasn't a permanent setup. She was thinking of someplace larger and with more possibilities, Seattle perhaps, or maybe Spokane. Women of her station didn't dream big, much less in Technicolor. But when she was under the influence of cheap sour mash, look out. She could be loud and abrasive with a whisky-soaked voice that brayed through the lobby like a P38 on takeoff, as Fox noted in October 1942:

Our man in uniform proceeded to cuss Everett hotels, and then went on to say that his job was to know the complete history of every officer out at the Field. There was something annoyingly smug and braggartly about the fellow. I felt it instantly, and Grace must have too, for she immediately began to question him about this and that person located at the Field–did he know Lieutenant So & So? Did he know Sergeant Blank? Did he know Corporal Blank Blank? To each query he could only reply "No, I do not—No, I don't know him," and so on.

"Hell!" she finally exploded, "I thought you said you knew all the officers out there!"

"Oh," was his excuse, "I only meant the commissioned ones—only the commissioned officers."

She took a long pull at her cigarette. "You know," she finally shot back, "I don't believe you're a soldier at all. I don't think you're anything but a God-damned phony."

This was pretty harsh stuff for any soldier to take, and more particularly for such a fellow as this egotistical wiseguy. "Yeah—what do you think I've got on this uniform for then? How do you figure that one out? How'd you think I got the uniform?"

But that one didn't stagger Gracie. "I'll bet you stole the uniform maybe. Yeah, by God! I'll bet anything I've got you simply took it from some guy, didn't you?"

By this time the other was beginning to see red. All of his previous calm self assurance had vanished in the heat.

"So I stole it? Well, I didn't steal it if you want to know. I don't want to boast, but I may as well tell you I enlisted to get it; and that's more than lots of these fifteen-dollar-a-day defense workers seem to care to do. And these WAAC's—there's a bunch of them out at the Field—all gettin' fifteen dollars a day and not worth a damn. I can prove I'm in the army"—he felt around his pockets and presently brought out his pass, and then came forth with an identification card, both of which he handed to Grace. She took them, glanced from one to the other. Waving them in front of her face like a fan, she laughed a high, strident laugh. "Hell, how do I know this name on here's yours—perhaps it belongs to some other guy that's layin' up somewheres drunk. I'll bet you probably took these from the same guy you took that uniform from. I'll bet a quarter on it, by Christ. Here's a quarter"—she handed me a two-bit piece—"now you give him a quarter an' we'll bet on it—these aren't yours at all, are they?"

Our hero was by now in high temper indeed—"By God," he exclaimed, "this's the first time I've ever been insulted by anyone like you. I'm going to get out and leave you to your funny ideas. I've always felt lots of these god-damned civilians don't give a damn about anything in uniform, but this is the first time I've ever had anyone tell me so in so many words."

"Yeah!" she came back. "Well, I don't give a damn either what you think of me. There's lots of girls not gettin' any fifteen dollars a day either. I'm one of them. By God I've always had to work hard enough for my living. 'Tisn't only you guys in uniform that's got it tough sometimes. I got plenty of my folks in the army and they don't go around boasting of all the officers' history they know, and peddle bunk like you do. You know what? I think you're full of damned bullshit myself—that's what I think."

I had meanwhile got the pass and identification card away from her and as the soldier started out the door ready to froth at the mouth I handed them back to him. I grinned at him and at Gracie. What the hell...

Army photographer Paul Alley had been one of the first to arrive in Everett, driving into town in a new 1941 Ford loaded with cameras and three other soldiers who joined him in the drive north from March Field in Riverside, California.

Rumor was it rained a lot in Everett, and each day enough lumber skidded out waterfront bandsaws to board up the entire state. Alley was from Arkansas, another young soldier in the car was from Mississippi, the other two from Oklahoma, all green as saplings. It was a late Saturday afternoon in May 1941 when they drove up Highway 99 past the last outskirts of Seattle, until there was nothing but fir trees and pavement and then Everett.

Alley took a reading of the place. The native rhododendrons bloomed huge raw blossoms of pink and violet that attracted scores of bees to the neighborhoods on Oakes and Wetmore. In a few hours, the sun would sink into the water beyond Whidbey Island west of Everett, turning the sky a streaky cinnamon red. At the same time, the air around the waterfront was a smudged-out gray from the papermill and sawmill smoke. The natural beauty of the setting and the industrial effluent that obscured it made a puzzling first impression.

He dumped his luggage into the three-story, downtown Everett YMCA across from the Armory, where he would work for a few months, while the Army Air Corps' Paine Field base on the outskirts of town grew from a city of tents to a permanent post.

Alley noticed colorful carnival posters nailed to telephone poles and taped to shop windows. After dinner he wandered over to the carnival, set up in a dusty field at the edge of downtown. As he approached, the noise grew loud and the smell of sweet candy washed over him—carmeled apples, taffy, and licorice twists. The soldiers in their pressed uniforms marveled at the strange-looking loggers wearing cork boots and dirty denim work pants cut off about mid-calf. The woodsmen had girlfriends who clung to them like bark on a tree. The soldiers and the loggers stared at each other, up and down. Alley wondered what sort of place this was, with its seagull-squawking waterfront and its mill workers, shop keepers, and fishermen living quietly, it seemed at first anyway, in blue-collar serenity. Then there were the mill owners and timber barons who slept in mansions on Rucker Hill and only rubbed elbows with their own. Everett was only 25 miles north of Seattle, but it was as if the big city down south had never touched this stubborn place.

At night the tops of sawmill waste burners circling the waterfront grew red-hot. Cinders became shooting stars, dodging through the protective screens and fizzling into the sky.

"It's the smell of money," the locals told newcomers when they complained of the sour egg smell that hung like a leaden cloud over the town of 30,000 residents. But even those women who were born here, and defended the waterfront smokestacks and sawmills as a God-given right to make an honest buck, were disgusted on wash day when the whites on their backyard clotheslines streaked black from drifting ash.

If you forgot and left a bedroom window open, by evening you'd have to shake the bedspread to rid it of sooty cinders.

The town Alley had blindly wandered into had four movie theaters. The Roxy, built in 1935 near the Strand Hotel, was showing *The Real Glory*, starring Gary Cooper. The Everett Theater, located almost directly across the street, was the town's showpiece movie house with 1,200 seats and gilded grillwork. Helen Hayes had appeared there many years earlier, as had Al Jolson, once with a vaudeville troupe, later as a full-fledged Broadway star. The Everett Theater was playing *Road to Zanzibar*, starring Bing Crosby, Bob Hope, and Dorothy Lamour. Admission was 35 cents, plus tax.

The robust taverns lining Hewitt Avenue downtown were open late into the night, although once the soldiers and the beer-guzzling war industry workers wandered off there wasn't much point in staying open. There were 46 taverns—30 on Hewitt Avenue alone. There also were 40 barbers, 8 butcher shops, 98 grocers, 43 lawyers, and 55 churches. There were only 3 booksellers.

A row of broken-down whorehouses huddled defiantly together at the less righteous end of Hewitt Avenue, and the painted ladies sometimes tapped-tapped a dime on their window panes, drawing the attention of prospective customers. Many an Everett lad heard the tapping and looked up to see one of those forbidden ladies smiling down from above. It was wicked, and exciting, too.

Alley didn't stay long at the carnival that night. Soon he was back in his YMCA room wondering about this rootless soldier's life and the strange towns it led to.

The next day he found a Baptist Church service more to his liking and the reception friendlier. The following week, after he'd been invited back to the church for Sunday school, Alley leaned over to a soldier sitting beside him, nodded in the direction of a pretty young woman, and whispered, "The little black haired girl, she's mine."

The woman, an Everett girl named Dorrie who worked at Chaffee's women's apparel store downtown, already had noticed the tall straight soldier from Arkansas cut impressively into his Army uniform. Their eyes met briefly. She never expected to see him again. Air Corps personnel moved in and out of Everett on trains and Army trucks without any particular regard towards the place. He was different from the others, though. There was something permanent about him, something that might understand and perhaps even appreciate the swirling tides and contradictions of her hometown. Everett grew into the marrow of your bones, if you let it.

Several months later on December 7, 1941, Alley and Dorrie, the little black haired girl, were driving north on the twisty two-lane highway to Mount Baker after Sunday school, when they heard an announcement over the car radio that made their blood run cold. It was 11:30 A.M. and the NBC radio network had just finished Sammy Kaye's Sunday Serenade.

"We interrupt this program," the announcer intoned urgently. "Dateline Pearl Harbor. The Japanese attack this morning..."

They decided if they were going to Mount Baker, they'd better hurry because the call was already out, all servicemen return to your bases. They arrived at the mountain; its peaks frosted with snow, snapped a few pictures for keepsakes, and hurried back to Everett.

Immediately after Pearl Harbor, the Army ordered a dim-out of all outdoor lights on the coast from Canada to Mexico to protect waterfront cities and U.S. ships from prowling Japanese submarines. Movie marquees, business signs, and floodlights from Vancouver, B.C., to San Diego were extinguished. Everett city workers fitted shields on traffic lights, so at night only slits for green and red were visible at street level.

Storeowners clicked off window lights that had shone as beacons of hope through the downtown's worst Depression years.

When the Army ordered blackout drills, drivers out on the roads crawled along by the glow of their parking lights. At home, even the bright slivers of light escaping through front door keyholes were dutifully taped over. More importantly to some, a few months later the dim-out order suspended nighttime Triple A baseball play of the regional favorite, the Seattle Rainiers, of the Pacific Coast League.

It wasn't long before even more young men with strange accents and curious ways flooded into the town by car, troop transport, and Great Northern passenger trains that hissed to a stop at the waterfront's Bond Street Station.

Trucks hauled soldiers over an alder- and fir-lined road southwest out to Paine Field, which to the big city boys seemed like light years from civilization. At night it was spooky the way the road cut through the forest—so dark and ancient, as if they were stepping back in time.

For two weeks after Pearl Harbor, soldiers were restricted to base and their girls waited for them to slip outside the gate for a few stolen moments together. By Christmas the restrictions eased. By February 1942, Alley and Dorothy were married.

In the 1920s, Ed Fox had read meters for the Puget Sound Gas Company. He was young then, and desperate to escape the sawmills that ringed Everett's waterfront. Reading meters not only earned him $125 a month, it freed him from a lifetime of working in sawdust. He learned something of Everett society as well, walking house-to-house over mansion lawns and weedy lots. But the real action in the '20s was the stock market and Fox, already a voracious reader with a prodigious memory, soon joined the fun.

"When I get to 50,000 dollars I'll quit the market," he told his cousin, Harry Dahl, and then set out doing just that. And damn near made it.

With uncharacteristic showiness and fistfuls of cash, Fox outfitted his ash-streaked house on Wetmore Avenue in fresh paint. Suddenly, he was a man without limits and so he splurged on expensive chairs, wallpaper, fringed lampshades, and an oak writing desk.

The young bachelor was up to $47,000 when the stock market crashed in 1929 and, like a lot of other investors, his fortune evaporated. If he learned anything from the lesson, it was to never again indulge in such an adventure.

So he burrowed in instead, once more scorning the sawmills, this time to write articles on finance at two cents a word for the *Broad Street Weekly* of New York. The paper folded. He bought a small press and began The Fox

The Strand Hotel on Everett's Colby Avenue, circa 1930. *Everett Public Library*

Head Press, reprinting small, limited edition, poetry books, a satisfying and spectacularly unprofitable flop. Everett wasn't ready for such sophistication.

One day, with funds running low and another great world war looming, Fox answered an ad for night clerk at the Strand Hotel, which sat unnoticed and unrepentant at the southern edge of downtown.

In time, Fox settled into the job, his eyes wide open, as evidenced in a letter to friend Russel in Edmonds.

Hello, old top!

I'm still at Ye Ancient Hostelry, night after night sitting reading while all respectable folk are snoozing & dreaming of things pleasant and delectable. Now and again my perusal of the printed word is rudely interrupted, by some sleepy transient, by some staggering drunk, or by some primeval male hot for a female to bed, or I might say, hot for a bed with female attached.

The other morning the bus driver out to the Field rushed in all asweat. Grabbing the phone he called the police station. Would they please hurry up with a "wagon" he had a girl in his bus so damned drunk she was stiff—he couldn't just chuck her onto the walk—a soldier had put her on out at the Field—would they please hurry as he was already ten minutes behind schedule!

In due time a patrol car appeared. The cop climbed into the bus very leisurely—all this was old stuff to him doubtless—walked over to where the girl was slouched, picked her up in his arms and carried her over to his car. She was just a kid, dead drunk. As the cop lifted her into the car her scanty little skirt caught on the door and was pulled up way over her waist, revealing all the poor thing had to reveal, which wasn't anything to become very excited about.

A number of people had gathered, and at this most of them began to laugh, although I noted that one man, middle-aged, quickly turned in disgust and walked rapidly away. A few of the women and girls contemplating this spectacle giggled and looked embarrassed, but most of them I think got quite a kick out of it all. So much for the new freedom for women! Circa 1942 the U.S.A. is as openly bawdy as was the Rome of Caius Petronius.

Steadily, old man, our old world is crumbling to pieces. Compared with today even the depression years seem not unpleasant. And the twenties very pleasant indeed...

The small, low-flying airplane circled the sun-dappled city as if gathering in something of the calm blue Puget Sound waters and the far-reaching Olympic and Cascade mountains. Then the pilot eased back and aimed his payload for the Snohomish County Courthouse's green lawn across from the Everett City Hall.

A crowd of several thousand looked up.

The war stamp booklets, spilling from the airplane like tiny, broken butterflies, sparked a mad scramble when they hit near the courthouse, which was built along the lines of an old Spanish mission. It was a warm summer evening, 6:45 Pacific War Time, and one-fifth of Everett squeezed onto the lawn awaiting the appearance of Constance Frances Marie Ockleman, better known as Veronica Lake.

Beautiful Veronica Lake—even her name implied something cool and mysterious. She was sultry and famous, a Hollywood star who managed to blur the distance between silver screen and small town dreams in a way that

Veronica Lake.

inspired hope. Still, this ashy Northwest mill town was a long way from Hollywood.

Lake's presence guaranteed success for the city's first Wings For Victory war bond rally. For days her name was on everyone's lips.

A crowd of nearly 6,000 assembled, some camped on chairs loaned from a local funeral home, while a backwater vaudeville show ground away on a portable stage and the Paine Field Army band harrumphed through a set of military marches. The brassy music drifted away and over Wetmore Avenue, hurrying up the late arrivals who heard it bouncing around in the distance. The adults lined up to buy war bonds at special tables assembled on an edge of grass, while women volunteers sat behind typewriters taking orders. The men, wearing airy summer straw hats that encouraged any stray breeze off the water, shouldered each other in friendly rivalry for position in front of a table, knowing that the first 30 would take home an autographed picture of the busty movie star. Every so often a volunteer ambled over and adjusted up the red line on a big wood thermometer standing alongside the tables. The adults murmured their approval. Eventually the thermometer showed pledges of more than $116,000.

At about that time across town, a Coast Guard boat pulled up to the Hewitt Avenue dock and out jumped a handful of smartly dressed sailors. They were more than anxious—practically falling over themselves—to help the pretty blonde woman off the boat and into the car that waited at the end of the wood planked dock.

When the shapely woman showed herself, Army medic Jim Tolnay aimed his camera and pressed the shutter release. Coast Guard sailors immediately surrounded him. One snatched the camera from his hands—a little too enthusiastically, Tolnay thought—opened the back, and ripped out the film, exposing the entire roll to the long-muted Northwest evening sunshine.

Taking pictures of military equipment, including that Coast Guard boat in the background, was off limits. Tolnay knew better. Now he stood and watched wistfully as the salacious sailors helped Veronica Lake into the Army car that disappeared up the hill towards the crowd at the courthouse.

Not far away, Ed Fox was home at 2102 Wetmore Avenue, reading or typing a long letter to Russel, the trusted pal in Edmonds. Their letters, the lifeblood of a long friendship, covered a generous amount of terrain, wildly changing course in several pages so that there might be a thought or two on Oscar Wilde, Franklin Roosevelt, a Russian novelist, or a *New Republic* article.

As he paused, looking out his second story bedroom window in the small house he shared with his mother, Fox observed the row of old maples standing guard over the neighborhood. They were like him, solid, ever watchful, blending into the landscape so that after a time you didn't notice they were there. Across the Snohomish River Valley rose the Cascade Range, and on a clear summer evening, when a marine wind blew the pulp smoke downsound towards Seattle and sparkling rays from the setting sun hit them just right, the peaks resembled church spires. Or devil horns.

Fox loved it here, but also chafed under the small town attitudes as well.

He once described himself as the sum of what he was not. He wasn't a hail-fellow well met, not a 500 percent patriot, not even a baseball fan. He was a free-roaming thinker who haunted dusty bookstores for stacks of socialist magazines and who despised the war's corporate profiteering and patriotic tripe. In his mind mankind was, despite its technological achievements, proving once again that it had advanced no further than the Middle Ages.

"To me, all wars are merely so many demonstrations of man's incurable imbecility; nations resorting to force either in offensive or defensive action indicate their people and their leaders are lacking in tolerance and understanding," he petulantly typed away in a letter to Russel. "I would do away with national pride and prejudices and the arrogance of intellectual smallbrains parading about in high places of state."

Sometimes on his day off, he'd be walking to a downtown newsstand when his cousin Harry, his only relative in town, would pass by and Fox, so deep in thought, wouldn't even nod hello. He wasn't, in short, the kind of fellow to join a pack of Everettites on a warm summer evening to welcome a famous movie star.

But there were events unfolding in town that no one, not even the most cynical, could ignore. In homes across Everett, families placed blue stars in front room windows, indicating to passersby that a son, daughter, husband, or father from that household was in military service. The blue stars were embossed or sewn on a background of trimmed, white cardboard or cloth.

The city's unit of the 161st Infantry Regiment, a National Guard outfit comprised in good measure of recently graduated Everett High School students—who joined up in the waning days of the Depression for prestige and free shoes—had been pressed into active duty. A stirring, flag-waving parade for them downtown, as they departed by train, began a journey that eventually took those Everett boys to dangerous South Pacific islands. Many who boarded the train that day were close friends and football heroes at Bagshaw Field. Some thought it all a marvelous adventure. Many never returned.

Whenever a graduate was killed, a gold star was added to the Everett High School service flag. Students also clipped out newspaper pictures of local servicemen who were training, promoted, transferred, or a casualty. The scrapbook at first was thin, but its deathlist grew: George Rankert, Jr.; Sebastian Vogel; Daniel Guisinger, Jr.; Gabriel Marcelle Hoflack; Winfred Oral Woods. Churches began posting pictures of Everett boys killed in the war, and their familiar eyes and growing numbers startled churchgoers on Sunday mornings. Gold stars, too, replaced some of the blue ones in the windowpanes of mourning households.

In the newspaper pictures taken before they left overseas, the smiling boys in fresh uniforms looked cocky, as if they alone had enough steel in the belly to deliver Tojo or Hitler a knockout punch. "Leave it to me, Ma," their faces seemed to say.

But when death notices began appearing regularly in the afternoon newspaper, a wave of worry began washing over town—the cream of Everett's future was dying overseas. The beginnings of such acknowledgment, however, were initially drowned under a tidal wave of patriotic boosterism. There was much to do and the enemy might be anywhere. Though threat of actual invasion diminished with time, there still remained fears of an enemy air or sea attack, or espionage.

Every so often there'd be a blackout drill, and Everett neighbors took turns, two at a time for a two-hour stretch, searching for offending cracks of light escaping from behind pulled-tight blackout curtains in houses tucked between thick-trunked trees and hedges.

Sometimes on crisp autumn evenings it was so foggy the neighborhood block wardens could hardly see their way and shivered a little from the eeriness as well as the chill. Nothing was so different as the familiar without light. Once as a block warden passed by a service station, an air hose fell and hissed like a rattler when striking the pavement. The poor man, just doing his patriotic duty, nearly jumped out of his shoes.

Neighbors met in living rooms with blackout curtains drawn tight and the kids tucked in bed to discuss how they'd handle a Japanese attack. They planned escape routes to eastern Washington through the protective Cascade Range.

Al and Irma Petershagen's two young children, both under age six, were taught to tie their own shoelaces to avoid any slowdowns in a frantic scramble out of town. The men would find their way over the mountains later, after they'd helped defend Everett, building by building, brick by brick. For a time the image seemed frighteningly possible: bloodthirsty Japanese soldiers in ugly green uniforms and hopelessly thick glasses swarming towards Everett City Hall.

Air raid shelters sprang up everywhere.

"Don't relax, don't grow complacent," warned Joe Blue, Everett's Defense Coordinator.

Still, the Army wasn't pleased with Everett. Following two nights of street-by-street inspections, a special Army team solemnly handed over a long list of dim-out violators. The most serious scofflaws were taverns, service stations, restaurants, and a few private homes that brazenly disobeyed the blackout orders.

The Army team herded Everett's civilian defense leaders into City Hall for an emergency meeting. The Army wasn't used to such insolence. "Take prompt, vigorous action, including arrests if necessary," they thundered.

Stung and embarrassed, Everett's civic leaders got going.

The next day, a front page story in the *Everett Daily Herald* reminded citizens that violations of the dim-out order was a public nuisance and they could receive a $25 fine or 90 days in jail.

When it came to war, Everett was going to show the Army it meant business. And if that business included buying war bonds, particularly if it was a summer evening with Veronica Lake, it would damn well buy war bonds—even if guys like Ed Fox didn't show up. Guys like that thought too much for their own good, anyway.

All at once, with the Paine Field brass band thumping away, the movie star arrived at the courthouse, smiling and waving. She was helped from the Army car and escorted to a stage where she was promptly handed a homemade cake. For a moment she was Constance Ockleman again. But then she gathered herself. Everett must've seemed very woodsy and smudged around the edges to Lake, who was at the peak of her fame.

So many women were imitating Lake's peekaboo hair, brushed over the right eye, that the government asked her to change hairstyles for the duration of the war. Across the country, female defense workers were snagging their Veronica Lake-styled hair in war plant machinery. The government was seldom denied anything on the homefront. She stood before Everett now with her famous blonde hair brushed back.

The crowd strained for a better view. *What would she say? There she is, there she is. Look how short she is.* The air seemed ready to explode. Some of the local women with their hands resting on baby carriages thought that with those expensive clothes, makeup, and styling, well, maybe they'd look that way too, and their hands subconsciously ran through their hair. Well, it wasn't that far-fetched.

The tinny speakers squawked annoyingly. Rather disappointingly, Lake said only a few words into the big stand-up microphone about buying War Bonds, and then, as if it had all been a dream, she was whisked away. Later it didn't matter what she'd said; Veronica Lake had shown up. Imagine that. Veronica Lake in Everett.

The chairs were packed up and returned to the funeral home, the electrical wires recoiled, the stage disassembled, and the sound truck rumbled off in a choking cloud of blue exhaust. It was dusk when the last of the crowd disappeared from the shadows growing alongside the courthouse lawn. In the distance the familiar hum of an airplane engine returned and crickets began tuning up their summer chorus. Small green weeds stubbornly pushed out from sidewalk cracks.

The crowd of civilians ambled off to their working class bungalows on Lombard and Rockefeller. Veronica Lake, her tour of duty in Everett not yet completed, was driven a few miles down Highway 99 to the Windmill Club, an old whiskey-soaked roadhouse on the outskirts of town. Inside, a private party for a Paine Field squadron awaited the big star.

When the door opened and Veronica Lake entered, the entire club stopped as if caught on film. She was directed to a booth where she was quickly pounced upon by men with beery breath, who leaned in close or boldly stretched an arm around her fragile shoulders while grinning friends snapped pictures. She was a swell sport, they told each other. A foamy pitcher of beer and several glasses appeared on her table. An 11-piece Paine Field Army dance band, propped up on folding chairs on a stage before a big American flag, began snapping out popular songs that cut fast through the smoky club.

The movie star stayed long enough to sign her name to several scraps of paper and gamely pose for more pictures, before escaping the noise and heat in a rush to Seattle.

Lake's new movie, *Sullivan's Travels*, with Joel McCrea, was opening the next day at the Balboa Theater, admission 23 cents.

The party at the Windmill was still going on when, across town, Ed Fox glanced at his wristwatch and saw it was nearing midnight. He departed the darkened house where his mother slept, and started out that summer night down Wetmore Avenue past the solitary maples and the empty high school (he'd lasted only half a year) before reaching the edge of downtown. He kept going, heading up past the closed shops and the still open working class saloons, the Blue Diamond, Cave, Castle, DeRoo's, Norm's, and the Martini. When a tavern door opened before quickly snapping shut, he heard the laughter and glimpsed the faintest wisp of bottles and cans standing before blurry barstool customers. At Jack Mann's, one dime bought a 16 oz. schooner, poured and delivered.

Fox was a tall man and thin. Thus his strides were long and strong, the kind you'd expect from a man accustomed to walking everywhere. The sound of his footsteps on the concrete sidewalk was absorbed by the night.

It was nine-tenths of a mile from home to the Strand Hotel, where he would settle in and take stock of the proceedings from the matronly swing shift clerk he secretly called Pruneface. There was a loud party forming up in room 23, and a soldier and some woman had sneaked into room 32. Oh yes, the hotel's owner wanted to be sure he gave the boot to any lobby loiterers. There'd be no free stays at the Strand Hotel this night.

Tell the world the night clerk had arrived.

Fox had been at once amused and troubled by what played out on the hotel's stage before him. If you totaled it up though and divided the pieces, you'd conclude he was perfectly content here among the overnight rabble.

"What right have you or I to go about telling others what they shall or shall not do?" he wrote. "If they choose to drink themselves into a triple case of D.T. obviously it's their own affair; ditto if they prefer to diddle until there's nothing left to diddle with."

Fox looked up from his book. As was his habit, he placed a finger inside as a marker so the book seemed to grow into a part of his hand.

Except for her small, shapely legs, there was nothing particular about Gracie to attract attention and yet he found himself drawn to her. She was unpretentious, honest in her own fashion, and stood her ground. Her favorite color was blue which, Fox discovered, often matched her mood.

During the war, Everett's nights were full of Gracies, unattached women who smoked cigarettes like men, drank without conscience, talked too loud, and earned their meager keep in the beer joints on Hewitt Avenue.

They were junkyard dogs who slunk away when the sun broke over the jagged Cascade peaks and respectable folks recaptured downtown.

In the Yukon Tavern, Gracie dutifully delivered Rainier beer to tough men who eyed her with little regard from the barroom stools on which they sat. They weren't kidding each other—she was a middle-aged bargirl and available cheap.

Gracie chased those rough men off their stools when the big electric clock behind the bar told her it was closing time. Outside the air was damp with the smell of pulp mill effluent boiling in huge tanks. The sound of oiled bandsaws that ripped through old-growth logs all night at waterfront mills seemed to tear up and down the streets as well. And yet at the same time it was peaceful here and small-town like, the sidewalks dark, but the Strand safe and never far away.

Then, Gracie and Fox often let the remainder of night slip into dawn. Sometimes they wandered upstairs to her sparse room.

Of all the unlikely hookups, theirs was the oddest indeed—Fox the bookworm, and Gracie the tough little Hewitt Avenue sparkplug. Theirs was the oddest of couplings indeed, but in the midst of war, when men and women entwined for no good reason other than easy availability, anything could happen and did. In doing so, Gracie shot closer to his heart than Fox cared admit.

It's astonishing how many people are lonesome, longing for at least some momentary companionship, in this world so full of people and so full of things to divert their senses. And the world seems full of nothing but trouble and sorrow instead.

Fox and Gracie climbed to her room up the tired old hotel stairs, polished clean in the last 26 years by the ghosts of a thousand couples. They exchanged pulls from a half-drained quart of Kinsey Whiskey that sat on a small desk by the bed. All at once she turned and kissed him long and hard. He could taste the whiskey on her tongue. She was lying soft and warm in his arms and he smelled her perfumed skin.

Suddenly she pushed him away.

"Ed, you know what I'd like to have from you sometime?"

"No. Unless it might be this," and he pinched her gently and laughed.

"No," she whispered. "No, not that. That's not what I mean anyway. What I'd like to have from you is a little wristwatch, and with the initials G from E, Grace from Ed."

5

Zero Ward, Cabanatuan

*T*here was this so-called hospital at Cabanatuan that you went to die. It was nicknamed Zero Ward. When you hit Zero Ward you were about gone from malaria or dysentery. Your life span was measured in days or hours. Zero was the end of the line.—Galen Martin

Army Medic Henry Chamberlain stirred from an uneasy sleep. Night cries were hardest to ignore.

The young medic forced himself to look out at what he didn't want to see. The flies, he noticed, also were awake in Zero Ward.

Daybreak streaked in gold filaments through the slats at one end of the long narrow building. Patients lay at floor level on bamboo shelves soiled in their own filth, and above them were additional identical rows of shelves and men, most without blankets.

They would die that way, of course, uncovered and miserable and there was nothing he could do, not even clean them of the diarrhea that occupied their last thoughts. Shelf after shelf of them settled there, vacant stares and zombie faces.

Alongside him on his own dirty little shelf sat a packet of rudimentary medical supplies that somehow had lasted this far into the war: a pair of bandage scissors, surgical needles, copper sulfate crystals, and a dab of glycerin. His grandfather's straight razor also survived and now bore witness to that unearthly place called Zero Ward.

Outside the sun splashed watercolor red over the Cordillera Central range, its rays brushing the virgin sky with tendrils soon breaching the Zambales Mountains.

Henry Chamberlain, U.S. Army medic.

The sun would climb higher and hotter, burning without limit down on Cabanatuan, the old Filipino Army camp built between mountain ranges on the low, flat valley floor. The army buildings blended into the landscape, open, spare, and uncomfortable.

Before day's end, dandelions and other weeds with the poor luck to spring up inside the big barbed-wire compound were plucked clean by starving men in filthy breechcloths and Nipa leaf hats. There was little to tell the men apart as they pecked at the hard ground for food.

Still, the sunrise was beautiful over the Cordillera peaks.

The weakest prisoners shuffled in or were carried to one end of the ward that late spring of 1942, and gradually advanced down the assembly line as others died off, providing evidence to a growing sense that everything was pre-destined here.

As for Henry, when war arrived in the Philippines a few months earlier he weighed 165 pounds on an average-sized frame. His youthful, friendly face had managed to absorb life's twists without turning hard. But an uncommon maturity burned in his eyes.

He'd lived mostly on his own since he was 14 years old when the Great Depression drove a stake through his family. His father's small business in Omaha, Nebraska, had gone under like the withered crops of those disconsolate farmers whose parched land stretched beyond all horizons. When your livelihood includes selling generators to dust bowl farmers and they can't make payments, you can't make payments either. So the family business broke apart and then so did the family.

Although barely more than a child himself, Henry learned about guile and hard work. If you had to eat dandelions or other weeds for a while, so be it. You figured out quickly what it took and then carried on without complaint.

Part of the reason we survived through the war was we survived through the Depression. We learned a lot of things in the Depression, how to eat various plants that were not normally grown as edible plants. We did the same things as prisoners. We went even farther and tried plants that we didn't know anything about and we sometimes got into trouble because of it. We got punished by the Japanese and got sick from some of them.—Henry Chamberlain

Zero Ward, ground zero, land of the flies. Henry pulled a blanket over his head, concentrating on his morning ration of plain white rice. Besides shielding him from the flies, the coarse blanket offered a momentary escape.

But his rice lived. Wriggling through his meal were a dozen or so inch-long white worms with tiny black heads. At first the prisoners picked out the disgusting intruders, but after a few weeks in Cabanatuan they closed their eyes and ate them as well, hoping for any sort of protein.

His skeleton body, having long ago used up any stored fat, ate away its own muscle and tissue now. He felt it turning inward, feeding off itself until one day there'd be nothing left but anger.

He knew the biology of starvation, how the body eats the glycogen stored in liver and muscles, the loss of protein, the spells of nausea. What he couldn't anticipate was hunger's mental toll. Food was all you thought about, all you cared for, it was your god, your savior, your lover.

He finished his meal and swallowed the last entrails from the mess kit tin. A stray mutt never licked a bowl cleaner.

The air inside the blanket was hot and muggy, but when Henry pulled it back he was shocked all over again. Nothing changed, it was all still there before him. His patients. His men. His responsibility. Dysentery was a curse. So too was that dark place in his mind that blocked all memory of how he arrived in this wicked place.

Henry's train trip to the Cabanatuan prison camp had vanished in a malarial fever. The small metal cattle car, stuffed with prisoners, clattered through cane fields, illusions in the edgeless heat.

Later, others told him of standing so sandwiched together they couldn't even wiggle a finger, still Japanese sentries used rifle butts to batter in more. Sour breath in no account faces. When someone filled with dysentery lost control, their liquid waste splashed down the legs and feet of others. Soon the steel boxcar floor wore a thin coat of human excrement that rolled and shifted as the car banked through curves. Some died standing up, and no one knew it until they offloaded at the Cabanatuan rail siding and corpses collapsed face down onto the slippery floor.

Henry's brain simply clicked off, sparing him such details.

When he awoke he was at Cabanatuan, lying in a building, covered with flies. He was all but dead except for an ember of life deep inside him, stoked by a defiant heat.

Following Bataan's surrender in April 1942, the Japanese had gathered up Henry and the other medical personnel from a huge American field hospital and delivered them to the ancient Bilibid Prison in Manila.

There was a dark, foreboding feel to the prison with its forlorn cellblocks and 20-foot high earthen walls.

Henry already was weak from an advanced case of jungle malaria; so when the cold metal doors of Bilibid clanged shut behind him, he felt swallowed up with defeat as if it were part of the malarial air he was forced to inhale.

He glanced nervously at the prison's depressing walls and felt a sudden chill. In doing so he muttered something aloud, a word, a phrase, a syllable of fevered despair.

At the sound an annoyed Japanese interpreter looked up from his paperwork and Henry felt a sharp, open-handed slap across his face. For weeks it'd been like that, humiliating and unfair. But the prisoners learned to accept such indignities with an impassive stare that saved them from further beatings. Except on this one day. Henry reached out and slapped back.

"Wrong, wrong move," he thought when the interpreter's surprised face twisted in anger. The air seemed to suck out of the place.

In a flash, two guards were on him, each holding an arm so for an instant he resembled a bony cross splayed out and exposed. The other prisoners stepped back and he became the main show, alone on stage. Anonymity was survival and he'd violated its most basic tenant. Now anything could happen.

The guards ripped off the remainder of his withered jungle uniform and began working their fists over his nakedness as if unleashing the fury of an entire army. They grunted methodically as they bent to their business. Henry was everything they hated about their American prisoners: pampered by luxury, white-skinned, and Western. They were unrepentant and dishonorable soldiers who chose surrender rather than death. If the Greater East Asia Co-Prosperity Sphere was to march forward on the backs of these unreliable Caucasians there would be trouble indeed.

The muffled sound of fist striking flesh thudded across the room. Soon his face was puffy and purple, and his ribs ached with every breath. But even that would've been tolerable if they'd left it there, left him alone to suffer and then recover. Through the pain of nearly swollen shut eyes, he saw another guard approach. He seemed unremarkable, dark-haired and small like the rest, except clenched between his teeth was a cigar, the tip burning bright red.

Henry fought their grip. The guards clasped tighter against his sudden strength, while out of the swirling struggle the cigar swung forward and ground into the gray flesh of his arm. His mind fogged with pain. Then the other arm. It burned with such ugly force that it stole his breath away. They weren't finished until that guard, crueler than all the rest, reached between Henry's legs and frayed the cigar deep into his manhood and he could smell his own burning flesh, awful and sure. As consciousness slipped away, an anger bore deep inside him and, like that smoldering wound, scarred him forever.

Finished with his Zero Ward breakfast, Henry uncurled his legs and found his homemade wooden shoes that the prisoners called clacks. His feet were unsteady and he held onto his shelf for a moment, waiting for his equilibrium to right itself. His wobbly legs were like those of a sailor returning dockside after months at sea. Tied around his waist was a thin cotton breechcloth pulled up between his legs. Any useable clothing from Zero Ward bodies, their last will and testament, was dispensed to other prisoners still hanging on. Mostly it was beggarly rags passed from one corpse to another.

Henry began his rounds every morning, curious to see what the night had brought, his hard uncomfortable shoes rubbing the tender skin of his feet and slapping the wooden floor. His patients, those still with minds, heard him coming, clack, clack, clack, like the echo in a tunnel. But without medicine—and the Japanese were providing none—there was little he could do.

He shuffled along the ward's narrow aisle and knew, with cold-blooded accuracy, which of his patients would die that day.

In the tropical air of the Philippines, an animal begins decomposing the instant it has drawn last breath. Sometimes, it seemed to the Zero Ward medics, the process began even earlier.

That's how Henry came to know the smell of death, a sickly stench that prophesized a man's last hours. A prisoner might still suck shallow reedy breaths as he lay face up on his bamboo shelf, but he already was gone. He didn't yet know it. The smell gave him away.

Every morning, Henry and the other medics portaged the bodies outside and stacked them in the sunshine, making room for others inside.

One out, one in. There wasn't much grieving over such basic mathematics, but the weight of the sum eventually ground everyone down.

Thirty to forty American prisoners died every day in the first three months at Cabanatuan, creating a logjam at the burial pits.

By mid-morning, details of ghostlike prisoners arrived outside the hospital wards, filling their litters with the weightless corpses awaiting them in the dirt. Even in death the Americans were out of place in the tropics, their long legs flopping off the sides of the litter, their heads lolling side to side.

When a burial detail reached the lip of a pit dug through the cogon grass just outside the camp's fences, they'd weakly deposit their burden, one emaciated cadaver atop another, completing a journey that began a forever ago in the great United States.

Eventually the weeks passed and warm monsoon rains burst open the skies over Cabanatuan, dumping torrents off the camp's thatched roofs. The burial pits became flooded brown lakes with fast drops pinging like bullets off the muddy water. Then, while one prisoner shoveled mud on top, another thrashed about inside the grave, holding down the arm or foot or head of a stubborn corpse that kept poking eerily out of the water.

Nothing smells like a dead human being. It seems to emit its own odor, different from anything else. A foul smell. We were constantly around that smell. So aside from the other smells there was the smell of death. Even those who weren't dead, who were comatose, would pick up that smell, start giving it off. You could tell someone was going to die from the smell.—Henry Chamberlain

Not far from Zero Ward, Private First Class Galen Martin held up his end of duty. In Cabanatuan the worst assignment of all was working a burial detail, but that was his lot and that was his duty. It was more than military discipline, though. It was human decency, something so basic he couldn't explain it beyond saying that burying your dead is what you do. Day after day, he carried those bodies along the same path worn through a field of grass past split trench "benjos" to the burial pits.

One day as he rested, Galen listened to the whispered chant of a chaplain softly praying over a tangled pile in the graves before him. It was a last call for spirits rising up and away from their earthly suffering. The sound was soothing, spiritual. The sun bore down upon the chaplain in such a way that he appeared almost angelic, an aura of goodness amidst the destruction.

A toe wiggled. The chaplain stared into the pit. A toe wiggled. Unbelievable. Galen hurried over and peered down. There, there, see it, the chaplain cried.

Galen couldn't trust his eyes, this was impossible. He scampered into the pit, stumbling over the legs and arms of others and found his miracle amid the honeycomb of bodies.

Minutes earlier they had carried that same young corpse away from Zero Ward, he with eyes blank, mouth slack. He was dead. No, he was alive!

They loaded him back on a litter for the only return trip Galen ever saw from the Cabanatuan burial fields.

Space was cleared on one of the hospital ward shelves. A medic poured a few ounces of watery soup through the man's cracked lips. Slowly life returned to him as if it were a kindling fire, gradually gaining strength. The next day he improved a little more.

He became something of a mascot, a symbol of hope at Cabanatuan. Every day when Galen returned for more bodies, he checked. Every day more of the man's strength returned. He shuffled. Then he walked. Word spread through the prison huts. About a month later, he was strong enough to walk himself back to the main camp. A Zero Ward escapee, how about that.

"You sure can rattle them death ropes," Galen said admiringly.

The prisoner returned the faint smile of someone who'd seen more than he should.

But now there was a nagging worry for those on burial detail. How many others had they buried alive?

In a rolling field across a gully not far from the Pampanga River, five Cabanatuan prisoners shoveled away the last of their lives.

The green grass brushed thigh high against the sun-browned men, and the clean wind shifted the grass about them side to side, so from inside the prison camp 150 yards away their movements seemed synchronized. But it was a deathwatch, and the grassy plain just another neutral uncaring landscape.

A few days earlier, the men had slipped away from Cabanatuan towards the inviting low brown hills on the edge of the horizon, where bands of Filipino guerillas operated against the Japanese. Their bruised faces told of their recapture. Heroes for a while, now they were sideshow freaks. For more than a day they sat in the blistering sun, their hands staked behind them in a field crawling with biting ants and wild dogs.

Jack Elkins glanced at them briefly through the squinty sunshine, but his attention remained on the chow line stretching before him. He wouldn't have let anyone slip in front, not even his best friend from back home. This was no movie lineup, no dime store checkout. There were no gentlemanly agreements here.

Behind him in the field, the five prisoners finished scraping their three-foot deep pits through the flinty soil.

The camp stopped and, as if one, focused out in the sunshine where a Japanese guard with a cap shielding his head also waited. At a signal his rifle rose. If you were to escape Cabanatuan, you'd better escape all the way.

A shot echoed through the camp's silent huts. One of the prisoners collapsed heavily in his grave by the rippling grass. The executioner's call repeated itself four more times, the sound ricocheting through camp each time, dusty and dead.

As the gunshots faded, a disturbing vision shook Jack, a vision so unvarnished it was like staring into the corona of his bared soul. Suddenly he saw himself from above, standing in the chow line with beggar pants and tattered shirt. From up there he could see how the remnants of civilization sloughed off him like a snake's molted skin. He saw Zero Ward, the dysentery huts, the starvation—half-dead men with grass hats staring at nothing.

He saw it all, but more than anything he saw how even the killing in the nearby field couldn't keep him from his place in the lineup to the thatched shelter, where rice gurgled in big black pots. He glanced again out to the field at the five bodies in the yellow afternoon, already nearly forgotten.

Here I stand in line for food, he thought. The moment passed. He reached out his mess tin toward the big black pot of rice.

A few weeks later, a Japanese guard led an old worn-out carabao inside the compound's barbed wire fences. The animal was used up, ready for scrap. In that way it wasn't unlike the prisoners themselves, who eagerly followed it in.

An excited pack soon surrounded the frightened animal and it was pulled along in their wake to a lone tree near a guard tower. The beast, eyes rolling with fear, was roped to the tree; its hooves planted defiantly in the dirt. Someone emerged through the mob holding an axe used for chopping wood.

But this was no woodpile and the carabao, even one as old as the Philippines itself, was a challenge. The axe blade merely glanced off the carabao's knotty skull. Another blow and a fine bloody mist seemed to rise from beneath the shady tree. A third and a fourth strike landed, but still the trembling carabao stood.

By now more than a hundred prisoners gathered, each hoping for a share of the prize. As the axe blade again glanced off the terrified beast, the crowd grew impatient. More men hurried over, attracted by the commotion, sharks smelling blood. Hurry, hurry, kill the beast. It'd been weeks since their last morsel of meat.

Finally a prisoner with a long cooking knife and the look of someone who knew how to use it elbowed through the crowd. Without a word he expertly slit the animal's stubborn leather throat, while blood dripped through his fingers and soaked into the ground. The carabao sighed. The mob attacked.

Jack emerged cradling the giant animal's head, its fatty yellow veins leaking blood, its stone eyes staring, its enormous tongue leading a tailwind of flies.

Surrounded by a handful of prisoners, who broke off and followed him, Jack gathered up a five gallon can, filled it with water, and built a fire. He knelt alongside, peeling back the hide and occasionally scraping the knife on the side of the pot so every useable glob of fat fell inside the boiling water, along with the tongue, the flesh, even the eyes.

He felt prehistoric, a cave man squatting by the world's first fire. The only rules worth having were those guaranteeing you'd see another day. And today it was a carabao skull that would see him through.

They gobbled everything out of that pot, even the bones, which boiled up soft enough to chew. Eventually all that was left were the stained brown teeth and Jack would've eaten those too if only, by God, they'd softened up right.

You become hardened to it. It happened early with me, I didn't think I'd get captured. I just knew I was going to be dead, there was no way I was going to make it off Corregidor. It took me several weeks to realize that "Hey, I'm still alive." This wasn't the way it was supposed to work and I was quite shocked. I wasn't prepared for this; living wasn't something I'd considered. You never get so you can just walk through death, it still bothered you, but you find that you become hardened to misery.—Jack Elkins

6

See ya' on Market Street

*F*REE OF CABANATUAN AND GOOD RIDDANCE.

Or so it seemed at first, until Jack and 297 others from the Filipino death camp found themselves lined up beside a squalid cargo ship bound for Japan in late fall 1942.

Now, into the jaws of the beast itself in the great East Asian war—Dai Toa Senso.

The year was snapping shut on six months' captivity with no word from home, no future beyond the next mouthful of stale rice. The POW grapevine that sizzled with rumors of American invasions and submarine rescues was strangely silent about what awaited in Japan.

The cargo ship's corroded steel hull did nothing to cool Jack's apprehension. He wondered how the freighter, which he reckoned about five hundred feet long in Manila's old harbor, managed to stay afloat.

It was an open sore that defied all laws of seaworthiness.

Now what, he wondered.

The metal railing leading down into the ship's hold felt moist from the palms of those ahead. Perhaps it was fear that made them sweat. Perhaps it was the suffocating darkness below that overwhelmed them before they even reached the last rung.

Down, down went his feet, each step further into the belly of it, until the light was snuffed out completely and all he had were the familiar tainted smells of human sweat and defecation.

Jack found the floor of the ship's bottom, and he stumbled forward over the shadowy outline of men packed so tight that there was hardly room to

Jerry Hanson, Yokohama prisoner #995.

step. His eyes, weakened from a six-month diet of water and rice, had trouble adjusting—perhaps they just didn't want to see.

He was thirsty and fighting off the rising panic of being enclosed in such a black scabrous place among so many hopeless men.

Steam like that from a swamp seemed to rise from sweat-soaked shirts. Men collapsed in the heat.

Squeezed in beside him was Jerry Hanson, a fellow Marine with a narrow, kindly face that Jack had met in boot camp and then knew in Shanghai before the war started. Hanson was several inches taller than most prisoners, and, like every starved one of them, had a waxy, corpselike complexion. Hanson occasionally had visited Jack's foxhole when the artillery let up on Corregidor and the two chatted out there

as if it were a Sunday social. Jack had liked him immediately. Later, after the American surrender, for some unexplainable reason Jack was drawn to him from the 6,000 prisoners on Corregidor waiting to leave for Cabanatuan. They sat together in the hot sun and shared rations. It was the start of a friendship soon tempered like blacksmith's steel in the heat of prison camp life.

Now onboard this hell ship bound for Japan, Jack was grateful for Hanson. Under the circumstances such human bonds might make the difference.

Jack Elkins, Yokohama prisoner #997.

The days thus blurred into one long seasick misery, only broken when the guards unscrewed the hatch cover and a circle of light pierced the darkness below and a swab of cool outside air bathed their faces. Almost immediately a tub of rice was hand-lowered out of the light, and dirty prisoners scurried like cockroaches to make room before it thunked on the metal floor. They wolfed down their food while the wood bucket rose back up into the circle of light. A few moments later it appeared again, half-filled with water.

Some prisoners wondered aloud if the rice bucket was the same that'd be lowered later for a toilet.

It would've surprised no one.

With the hatch open, the prisoners bound the bodies of their dead comrades with rope and one by one they rose toward the light, twisting and slamming into the stained sides of the cargo hold. Mumble a prayer, say goodbye. Up top the bodies floated a few seconds on the tossing waves before disappearing under the ship's wake. The ocean was endless and harsh, a graveyard of unquenchable thirst.

The vessel creaked toward Japan. The air temperature dropped. Now instead of the incessant heat, the war prisoners shivered in their tropical clothes.

Those with enough strength occasionally climbed up from the hold in packs of 10 to sniff the fresh breeze topside and hang their skinny butts over the cold rusty railing to defecate—all under the watchful eyes of Japanese machine guns from a deck above.

Most prisoners hadn't the strength to climb up, but those who did witnessed a sight that grew more curious each day. Strapped to a deck railing was a prisoner with such an outward display of guts that even the toughest in the wallows below were amazed.

He was a loud, strong-willed Texan named Joe Gear, who was so weakened by dysentery he couldn't even walk down the ladder into the hold. He didn't have much life, but his grip on what little he had was startling.

At the start of the voyage, Hanson, who had a penchant for spotting others in a worse-off way, co-opted Jack into jerry-rigging a platform for Gear. Together they tied a 2 x12 plank to a bottom railing, another they braced on the deck. Onto this arrangement they tied Gear, first removing his shit-soiled pants and then covering his shirt and coat with a green army poncho. Having done all they could, they left him alone on deck to roll and pitch atop the ocean's white capped swells.

Every morning when Jack inched up the last step of the ladder and poked his head onto the deck, he expected Gear to be dead. It was only a matter of time before Hanson's latest experiment in humanity would fail, and they'd unstrap the Texan and let his body slide off the plank into the ocean.

But every sunrise was a beginning. Joe Gear lived. So they carried up what few grains of rice they could spare and forced it down his throat with a gulp or two of water. Then, while Jack held up his legs, Hanson poured a bucket of seawater over the plank and then on the man's diarrhea crusted legs. Gear shook in their grip. The November wind blew in their faces.

He was a tough buzzard, slow to die. For two weeks Gear shivered alone on the wooden plank through the cloudy days and starry nights, his poncho howling about him.

He was still up there when the freighter creaked into Japan and the prisoners filed weakly up and out of their nightmare and past him, still strapped to the planks. The guards refused Hanson's request to bring him along. He was too close to death, the guards decided. He'd be useless as a slave laborer.

And so Jack and Hanson untied Gear from the planks and gently laid him on the wide busy dock alongside a pile of corpses pulled from the freighter's hold.

They explained to Gear that this was the end of the line, that he'd be left there on the dock in his green poncho. Then, they turned to join the rest of the prisoners climbing aboard trucks that awaited them dockside.

"See ya' on Market Street," Gear's voice drifted out gamely from somewhere inside the stack of bodies. Hanson and Jack turned into the hard Japanese winter. San Francisco was the last place they expected to run across Joe Gear. In their next life, perhaps.

The bumpy ride in the open Japanese truck shook Jack's insides until it felt like his organs had shifted. The drab Asian city passed by and he absorbed the stares of the Yokohama civilians in their blouses and winter coats. The crooked wood buildings, grown together on narrow streets, reminded him of

Shanghai. There were open markets and vegetable stands with cabbages and row after row of daikon, their long white radishes. Later, the prisoners would joke that all it would take to end this war was for the big American warplanes to start bombing the daikon fields. No daikon, no war.

Above the storefronts with the strange Kanji letters lived families behind rice paper walls. It was all so mysterious and depressing. The smell of raw fish clung to the streets. Fat-tubed bicycles rested in racks. Hidden among all those buildings, as far back as the eye could see, were small factories pumping out war machinery parts.

The ride, deeper and deeper into the confusing maze, ground on into Yokohama's industrial waterfront, and now it was the smell of industry that drifted into the truck. At the waterfront, Japanese warships were riveted together in the gloom—welding arcs sprayed gold sparks across the enormous docks where joyless men and women and even their children scurried about.

The damp, salty wind bit at Jack's face and seemed to gnaw through his tropical clothes. His blood felt thin after all those months in the Filipino heat and it wouldn't have surprised him now if chilled water flowed through his veins.

Eventually the caravan of trucks braked outside an oversized wooden warehouse ringed by a canal and barbed wire. Jack surveyed his surroundings.

A cold breeze blew across the beachfront and with it the pungent odor of kelp.

As befitting their status as slave laborers, the prisoners were to live like animals in the drafty, barn-like warehouse. Without even stepping inside, Jack knew it would be without comforts. With more men pressed into military service, the need for labor in the Japanese war factories was critical. The effort now included captured Allied prisoners, who reluctantly joined the thousands of civilians building Japanese arms. But whatever the enemy gained in forced labor they lost in sabotage, an equation the Japanese military never seemed to grasp.

An eight-foot-high chain link fence topped with strands of razor-sharp barbed wire surrounded the prison. At night, big overhead spotlights cast down on the camp and the barbed wire gleamed menacingly.

Jack was about to enter the warehouse when he heard his name.

"Hey Jack, Jack, Jack." It was Hanson's rapid-fire voice. He turned.

Hanson's arms were draped around a sorry looking prisoner who sagged under the weight of his pack. Another of Hanson's projects. Another Joe Gear. Jack dropped his duffel sack and helped shoulder the fellow to the end of a line of POWs waiting in front of the warehouse. Slowly the line began moving. It didn't seem to matter which army or which country he was in, there were always lines. And now he found himself at the end of another one. First in line, last in line, he couldn't win, not since Corregidor, not since the surrender.

The prisoner was Fred Johannsen, a tall young soldier whose bruised body showed the strain of prison camp life. He was nearly finished. The hell ship and months of hunger had about done him in. But there was a spark of life in him yet and now he had Hanson and Jack on his side. Together they struggled inside the big barracks to where a Japanese guard sat at a table passing out numbers and writing down names: Hanson 995, Johannsen 996, and Elkins 997. Jack was the last prisoner through the door, the last man to take stock of his surroundings. He was familiar with disappointment and so what he saw didn't shock him.

The big open building had a wide concrete center aisle and, in anticipation of their arrival, Japanese carpenters had built up narrow, wooden sleeping shelves along either side. The first level was three feet off the ground, the upper bays about seven. Wood ladders led to the top shelves.

The Japanese had made accommodations for a thousand prisoners, each with a space about three feet wide and eight feet long. The sides of the warehouse, dark around the edges where the lights never touched, were chicken wire and stucco.

Johannsen, Hanson, and Jack would live 30 inches apart in a flea-infested upper bay. Eventually Jack would know them better than his own brothers. He'd know all about their growing up, could tell you about their families, their aspirations and disappointments, as if they were his own. He'd know that Johannsen once lived in an orphanage, and at night curled up like a child in the blankets at the bottom of his sleeping bay. Jack would rely on kindhearted Hanson as he would no other.

He threw his sack up before him, climbed up to his bay, and from that height surveyed his new surroundings. Jack, now forever stamped prisoner 997, could feel the damp air stealing his strength.

The sounds were everywhere, strange whispered sighs from men wrapped in coarse blanket cocoons. They were weak as newborns and he was no better.

Jack tucked his arms down between his legs for warmth, but it was a cruel joke. He was so starved that his arms slid right on through past the elbow, a wishbone with the meat picked clean. Sometimes he couldn't believe they were *his* legs.

The gray Japanese winter discovered chinks in the old waterfront warehouse, and the cold knifed through each cocoon until the bundle inside was all but gone.

Glare from a yellow light shining overhead never let up and if Jack opened his eyes he knew what he'd see. There'd be row upon row of men just like him on hard wooden shelves, nearly a thousand in all, toe-to-head, side-to-side, skinny, and starved. If he'd sat up on one elbow and stared into the faces, he'd see himself reflected a thousand times—cordwood corpses waiting to be hauled off and burned.

He could close his eyes and shut it out; he could shut out the small, cruel Japanese guard on nightly rounds who strutted stiff-backed between the shelves of matchstick prisoners. He could shut out the image of strong young men melting away until only their eyes showed dark and brooding in look-alike faces. He could do all that, but he couldn't shut out the sounds.

The moans of dying men were enough to turn his stomach.

Jack was a tough Corrigedor Marine who knew what it meant to sight down on the enemy up close, and yet he could feel his body betraying him, wasting away with dysentery chills that started somewhere in his core and worked out until they froze every pore. It was as if he were drifting away in a winter fog.

Others were drifting away too. Their death chants spread across the unheated warehouse, a reminder of his own weakness, like the emptiness in his belly.

Why don't they hurry up and die, he thought. And after having thought it he didn't feel mean or guilty. He just was, that's all.

It was the dawning of Christmas 1942. Jack weighed less than 100 pounds. Christmas was a Pacific Ocean away, and fading like all the rest into a blurred memory of small town Friday nights and perfumed girlfriends in warm backseats.

Already it was forever gone.

Hanson bent over him, forcing a spoonful of rice into Jack's unwilling mouth. For a moment, Hanson's face blocked the harsh yellow light overhead. Few loners survived. Without a buddy—someone like Hanson to look after you, to make you eat when you were too weak to swallow—you were gone.

When a man died in this prison camp, the corpse was cremated and the remains poured into a pine box about a foot square to be shipped home, although the prisoners knew it never would happen. The boxes were stacked on top of each other in plain view, a kind of macabre tracking system to remind the prisoners of how they were doing. When he opened his eyes, Jack could see the boxes, piled up to nearly 100.

"Don't you die on me," Hanson whispered.

7

Where am I for God's sake?
(Everett, 1943)

*A*GENTLE MIST SETTLED IN, blurring the horizon so that Hat Island, three miles west of Everett across Puget Sound, was lonely and mysterious. Every so often a P38 Lightning broke free of the gray overcast and dove for the island, pelting soggy beachhead logs with machine gun fire before pulling up and vanishing back into the clouds.

Medic Jim Tolnay and a crew of three watched the attacking planes from the deck of a 40-foot-long Army Air Corps crash boat. If one of those planes with its eager young pilots came down, and they sometimes did, Tolnay was ready.

In the last few months, the medic helped rescue two Army training pilots from the cold water and another who ran out of fuel and ditched his plane on a rock-cobbled beach near town. When he'd paddled over in the crash boat's skiff, Tolnay discovered the pilot had plenty of fuel, had simply forgotten to switch to an auxiliary tank.

Not long after the start of the war, a P38 pilot bailed out over the Sound and his plane, as if guided by its own free will, suddenly veered towards Everett and exploded into a house on Grand Avenue. The house was empty that Sunday morning, the widow away visiting her daughter in Yakima. Big pieces of siding, broken tree branches, and airplane parts smoldered halfway down the block.

Three weeks later another plane from Paine Field sputtered down, this time into a chicken farm on the southern outskirts of Everett. It was a raw winter evening and the plane, on a routine training flight—as the government always claimed—narrowly missed two homes, struck a chicken house

P38 crackup near Everett, Washington, May 2, 1942. *Snohomish County Museum*

at high speed, and burst into flames that killed more than 500 chickens and licked high above the nearby fir and alder trees. The pilot's parachute popped open and he drifted safely into the darkened city below.

At parachute height and descending, Everett must have appeared a gloomy, half-lit place. The waters of Puget Sound to the west were black and the surrounding forests thick and primitive. It was a place closed in by nature and some of the fliers from America's open prairies felt constricted by it.

In the darkness just east of town, huge peat bogs resembled patches of fungus. A man could get swallowed up in those bogs and never be heard from again. Then again, he could just leave on a troop transport overseas and never give the place another thought.

Across the way, the P38s continued their machine gun attacks on the beaches of Hat Island. The sound was muffled, absorbed by soggy rain clouds hanging so low they appeared to snag in the treetops. Nobody paid much notice to the Paine Field fighters anymore. This day, after all, was becoming like any other in Everett.

The city had developed into the busiest hub of activity between Vancouver, Canada, and Seattle. There were grocery, furniture, and department stores, butcher shops, dentists, doctors, pool halls, and grease-splattered repair shops that coaxed overworked automobiles through the war. Detroit factories hummed with the patriotic, not to mention profitable, business of building army tanks, not roadsters for hotshots left behind.

The government set the nation's speed limit at 35 mph to save tires and, as it had since the start of the war, gasoline was tightly rationed.

Those sorts of hardships passed unnoticed by Ed Fox, who had neither license nor car, and rarely left Everett.

"What would I want to see of the world?" he once remarked to his cousin, Harry. "I've got my books."

And besides, the world was coming to him.

The sidewalks of Hewitt and Colby were crowded with mothers pushing baby buggies past old and middle-aged men, anxious children lining up for their movie matinees, and sailors whose battle-scarred vessels limped into the Everett Pacific Shipbuilding and Dry Dock Company.

Men from every corner and hillock of the nation stood in twos and threes, lazily smoking cigarettes and eyeballing women who waited at Chaffee's to purchase what scarce nylons were available. In a military town, the line between marriage and divorce was somewhat blurry. Throughout Snohomish County in 1943 there were 505 divorces, double the number from a decade earlier. Parents, solid in their old-fashioned beliefs, shook their heads.

Also beginning to putter self-consciously around the city's busy downtown area were scarred war veterans. They were much too young to be so old. Most everyone tried not to stare, but it was hard not to. Here were hideously damaged men: faces fried in tank explosions or legs serrated by flying shells. Others appeared whole on the outside, but they had cloudy eyes and wounds running as deep inside as granite fissures.

"The first fruits of the war are coming home to roost—if such a mix-up of metaphors may be pardoned," Fox observed. "The discharged soldiers we see are of course relatively mild cases; I daresay some of those we don't see (and perhaps never will) would make the most cold-blooded of us gasp. In the hotel they appear almost daily, thin, hollow-cheeked ghosts of the laughing young men who went away not so long ago full of cockiness and nonsense. Not a few are mainly mental cases, nervous, depressed, and unable to sleep. Hanging around the lobby in their worn, shabby clothing, they present a curious contrast to the soldiers who have not yet seen active service."

When Fox passed groups of laughing soldiers leaning against downtown lampposts, he saw skeletons and gravestones.

Before the war, it took Al Petershagen, a rangy, handsome man with a wife and two young children, 45 minutes to walk to the bank and back from his insurance office near the Strand Hotel.

The errand, past the Owl Drugstore and the J.J. Newberry dimestore with its 50 cent lunch counter, passed quickly enough except for all those interruptions to chat and say good day. But the town had grown by 5,000 souls since the start of the war, and eventually Petershagen noticed there were more strangers than friends on the busy sidewalks and the hellos fewer and less friendly. It was the price of prosperity and not everyone thought it good.

Down by the Snohomish River where wild cattails and marsh grass grew, the Washington Stove Works abruptly quit building kitchen stoves. Instead, hundreds of workers, including women for the first time, bucked out ranges for the galleys of fast new Navy ships. Government contracts were everywhere, as common as driftwood.

The Everett Pacific Shipbuilding and Dry Dock Company had sprung up at the waterfront and delivered floating dry-docks that followed Navy fleets into battle. The company also began repairing war-damaged vessels, employing 5,500 and filling the streets with off-duty sailors and defense workers with lunch buckets tucked under their arms. Derrick barges, huge steel contraptions mightier than the ancient cedars that once defined Everett, overgrew the harbor skyline.

The start of waterfront shifts had to be staggered in the morning to relieve traffic congestion, a strange new pairing of words.

At the same time, the Boeing Company opened an Everett plant in a two-story brick building at the edge of downtown to build B17 Flying Fortress bomber parts that were trucked 25 miles to Seattle for assembly. Later, when the B17 was replaced by the B29 Superfortress, the airplane company opened a second assembly plant in Everett, a three-story operation with a machine shop on the first floor and wing assembly on the third.

There were more jobs than workers. The old-timers never saw anything like it.

July Fourth parade on Everett's Hewitt Avenue, 1943. *Snohomish County Museum*

At about that time, a 2,000 pound bomb from the Ordnance Division at Paine Field was loaned to Everett civil defense leaders. For the price of a $25 war bond, Everettites were invited to autograph the bomb, thereby impressing their neighbors and sending a personalized message to Tojo.

Soon the bomb, a fat gray ugly thing displayed in the lobby of the Everett Theater and then the first floor of the Rumbaugh-MacLain department store, was so covered with signatures it resembled a get-well card from parishioners to the pastor.

When moviegoers and shoppers stopped to inspect the bomb at close range, however, they were surprised at first. Then they giggled. The men pointed and laughed out loud, but their wives didn't find it so funny. Soon the whole town knew. Standing out in bold signature amongst the respectable names in Everett was the autograph of Lillie Stump, the city's best known prostitute and madam of the once notorious Kentucky Bar & Hotel.

It would make a family man like Petershagen wonder what was happening to his old hometown.

One day Fox was startled by a long forgotten face that stopped him in his tracks. It was a woman who left Everett 20 years earlier and had moved to Portland, Oregon, 150 miles south. She carried herself upright and proper, and was fashioned in the expensive fur and silks of someone who'd found a comfortable station in life.

One glance told him she was the kind of woman who'd disapprove of Gracie and her kind, the barmaids, waitresses, and chippies occupying Everett's nights. But even with her nice car and soft lifestyle, she hadn't escaped the war. Fox saw that as well.

I studied her face, noted the little lines deepening about the eyes, despite the excellent make-up she had, and noted especially the definitely graying hair. Finally she noticed my look—"You're counting all my gray hairs," she laughed. "I've put on most of them in the last six months—don't let them tell you worry doesn't give one gray hair, for I know better."'

"Worry?" I asked.

She told me then that Donny Junior is a prisoner of the Japs—had been rather seriously wounded in action, too. "Remember," she went on, "how you used to say

WACs march past the review stand, July 4, 1943; note the Strand Hotel at left, down Colby Avenue. *Snohomish County Museum*

that you never wanted to raise kids to be butchered in the next war? I hated you then for being so cynical, so awfully bitter about things. But I guess maybe you were right. Really, what is the use of it—you know, if anything should—if Donny should—should not come back ever, I don't think I could take it. I've decided I should just end it, right then."

As they parted on that Everett street, Fox too must have sensed that his own carefully constructed world was about to be tested.

By the spring of 1943, Gracie's talk of leaving turned serious. Seattle was less than an hour's bus ride away with its brick skyscrapers and block-long department stores. Its Union Street Station on the southern edge of downtown bustled with soldiers, businessmen, and wives herding about young children in a way that made Everett's Bond Street station seem slow and small town. Seattle was a place to lose yourself; Everett a reason to leave.

"Her eyes have a worried expression. At forty she's worn down by life more than most women," Fox said. "I daresay she's been hurt so much that she has become suspicious and bitter."

Fox hadn't forgotten his promise to buy Gracie a wristwatch, but so far hadn't done so, perhaps hoping to delay her inevitable tidepull downsound.

Restless and unhappy, Gracie switched jobs, deserting the Yukon for the Eagles, and finally the Imperial Tavern.

He waited her out, scrounging deeper into piles of dusty hardbacks and periodicals in Jeff's used bookstore, a mad apparition in his suit coat and bow tie. Fox had a bibliophile's eye for literature and a printer's acumen about a book well made. But he didn't collect books for resale or profit; he had the heart of a librarian. He wrapped himself in them for comfort, for knowledge, for their one-way ticket beyond the town he couldn't leave.

And so his collection grew into the thousands. The hard-backed books, Shelley, Keats, James Joyce, architecture, printing, and music sprouted like tropical plants around him at home and it was becoming a challenge to move around the piles.

But there was an orderliness to the amazing collection that mirrored the complications in his mind. The most important books were close by in his crowded bedroom, his innermost sanctum. Within arm's reach from the bed was a nightstand piled high with his prized Oscar Wilde's. Volumes less worthy were buried downstairs deeper into the maze. Still, Fox could lay his hands on any book in his library in minutes. He once wrote,

Books are the most satisfying companions I know of. I'm not saying that I do not like the companionship of people, both men and women, but when you most want them to be with you they are someplace else generally, or they can't stay as long as you want them to, and so on. But my books—there they stand, always ready to serve whatever mood I may happen to be in at the moment, remaining with me as long as I like. My library, such as it is, thus gives a key to my many moods no less than to my various interests. There is nothing in it dealing with such matters as blacksmithing, spring plowing or the proceedings of the United States Chamber of Commerce, simply because I am not interested in those things. On my shelves, however, you can find a volume on paper making, several on typography, the works of Thomas Paine, a few books on Rome & its history (including Gibbon of course), a bulky history of Prostitution, numerous books by or concerning such fellows as Frank Harris, Oscar Wilde, Edgar Allan Poe, Walt Whitman. And there stands Balzac in 18 gaudily-bound volumes, a set of Casanova translated by Machen, the Temple Shakespeare—plain but satisfying edition in twelve volumes, and of course Villon, Rabelais (in two different translations), Aristophanes and The Decameron.

As the war continued, so did the night clerk's correspondence. His letters grew more sprawling, more detailed, as if he needed to chronicle the era for generations to come. Welcome to the Strand, he seemed to say. Welcome to Everett.

Came about 4:30 a.m. A door banged somewheres upstairs. Sound of someone coming down the stairs, slowly, uncertainly, in a stumbling fashion. Finally, in the turn of the stairway into the lobby appeared our little Pumpkin, Helen, herself. Wearing pajamas and slippers.

"Well, well," I laughed, "look who's up & around & down here!"

"Yeh—look who is," Helen replied. "And Christ am I skunker than a drunk!"

She sat down heavily near the bottom of the stairs, her legs spread wide apart, her hands grasping the edge of the stair-tread. Her face was very red, her eyes half closed. She appeared just about ready to do a passout. At last she looked up at me, squinting from the light.

"Ed," she asked "Will you do something for me? You know that little soldier went up with me tonight? He's got to be out to camp by six o'clock. He's got to catch that 5:30 bus or he'll be in a spot. He's laying up there—passed out I guess, and I can't get him out—guess I'm kinda slippin' or something—can't take it anymore or something."

"Doesn't seem that your pal could take it either," I remarked, walking over to where she sat.

"Ah, that crazy bastard!" exclaimed Helen in disgust.

"You know what? He's been layin' up there drinking that god-damned rum and my whiskey and shooting his arm full of dope with a needle. Christ! That guy couldn't raise a hardon in a week of Sundays!"

I promised to go up and see what the hell I could do with Chuck. I opened the door to Helen's room, in which the lights were all on bright as a Christmas tree. On the bed, spread on his back and clad only in his shorts, was Chuck. His face was dead white and indeed he suggested more a corpse than a living person. I noticed several red punctures on either wrist, but saw no needle lying about. I shook him, shook him again and shouted in his ear. He stirred slightly; I shook him hard once more and he suddenly upped in the bed to a sitting position. "What!—Where am I for God's sake?" he wanted to know. He looked up at me, wondering who I was. I told him to get up and dress, he'd just have time to make his bus!

"Who in the hell are you, anyway?" he asked. "I'm not getting out until I want to, see!"

I said I didn't give a damn what he thought, but to get the hell up and dress. I helped him, for he staggered about all the time, hitting against the furniture and falling over chairs. He'd drop the various pieces of clothing I handed him, all the while damning the army and the girl who had brought him up to this room and got him stinko drunk.

"I don't care what you say," he shouted almost in tears, "I don't give a damn what you say—that girl's nothing but a damned chippy—a dirty damned chippy."

All the while I kept reminding him that it was getting late, that his bus was soon due and he had to make camp by six o'clock. After arguing some more, he suddenly became a most contrite person, begging my forgiveness, shaking my hand and all that. After an age we were finally ready to depart, he with his pockets full of bottles and getting sicker every minute. He was a sorry looking soldier, sitting *there slumped over and crying. He was shipping out that morning. He might never see anybody he knew ever again—his friends, his parents, no one.*

"Ed," he said finally, "you know—the war's a terrible thing—all these fellows going out and getting shot to pieces, worse than what they do to animals."

I looked at him a long time, this young soldier, afraid of what lay ahead, lonely, and right now drunk and awfully sick. His bus failed to appear, and as the time was getting uncomfortably near six o'clock I at last suggested that Chuck take a taxi out to the field.

Although I offered to pay his fare (he being without any more than a quarter), he refused my offer, damning all taxi cabs as robbers, and saying that he'd go to hell first. He began to throw up, and I rushed him over to the waste basket. But at about five to six he suddenly arose from his chair and staggered toward the door. I helped him out to the walk. One of the rum bottles fell from his raincoat pocket, crashing on the cement, the liquor quickly washing away with the driving rain.

He floundered a few steps through the wet morning, lurched against a plate glass front and sagged into a heap on the flooded entrance-way. He began throwing up, the mess running down the front of him.

I picked him up, again urging him to wait for a cab. This he obstinately refused.

"Oh Christ, Ed, but I'm sick. I don't know if I'll ever get there or not, but I'll try—I'll try."

I helped him along for a few steps, to the corner.

"Thanks—thanks Ed—sorry I've been such a bother. I wish I was dead."

He grasped the railing that runs along the walk at that point, over a basement entrance, and then staggered away down Wall Street, finally losing himself to my sight in the rain and the dark.

I hurried back to the hotel...

It was nearly Christmas day when Fox visited a downtown jewelry store and, looking over the glinting array spread before him, asked about a watch that caught his eye.

He picked it up and held it in his soft writer's hands, studying it closely. It was a Parker lady's wristwatch in pink gold with matching bracelet. The face shone with gold numerals in a block design. Perfect. A rare find indeed.

There wasn't time for an inscription and he hurried along the jeweler, who was slow in finding a box.

Late afternoon fell over downtown when Fox retreated from the jewelry store. Head bowed in serious thought, he passed row after row of small Everett businesses that advertised their meager wartime wares in the simplest terms: "Eat," the sign outside one greasy all-night cafe shouted; "Singer," called the sewing shop; "Telegraph," offered another.

The Rumbaugh-McLain department store display windows were filled with children's Christmas toys: a Mickey Mouse doll, wood tug boat, red fire truck, pop gun, tricycle, and play vacuum. A fat Santa in red suit with black trim worked through a lineup of squirming kids. Every radio in town, it seemed, was tuned to Bing Crosby crooning "I'm Dreaming of a White Christmas," a melancholy sentiment for those with sweethearts overseas.

Just like the ones I used to know.
Where the treetops glisten,
And children listen
To hear sleigh bells in the snow.

Knots of tough-looking men lurked outside beer parlor doors.

Fox knew his streets like a farmer knows his fields—Jeff's Book Store, the way Hewitt Avenue humped in the middle and drifted down both ends to the water, the 700 parking meters downtown, and the ratchet grind of grocers' delivery trucks gearing down around potholes backed up with rainwater. He knew how it felt to sink ankle deep in muddy, unpaved side streets. He knew Sunday mornings a long time ago when walking in the sunshine under the gaze of Mount Pilchuck with his cousin, Harry. They walked with fishing rods in hand towards Lake Stevens through cattail marshes. They discussed great literature, Fox talking most.

Gracie was gone from Everett; Gracie escaped from Everett.

A quick side turn down Rucker Avenue brought lightning flashes of his earliest days in Everett. There was the Dearle residence, old-fashioned, comfortable, and roomy, where the shadow of a flaxen-haired schoolgirl sometimes drifted like a ghost past the windows. The house eventually was sold to an adventuresome boozer, who once entertained a late night theater crowd by bellowing loudly and then puking atop the hood of his parked automobile. Across from the Dearle house lived the owner of the Owl Drug with his duchess-like wife, his sons, his three-car garage, and bootleg gin set-ups in every room. A few steps to the right and up from the sidewalk about 10 feet was the large brick bungalow where the superintendent of Everett Pulp and Paper lived decades earlier with his generous salary and charming wife. They employed a Negro gardener, a tall, powerful man who told bawdy stories with great gusto.

"You know…," he once boomed at young Ed Fox who was working his way between houses on his meter reading route for the gas company. The man was leaning on a shovel staring at Fox's shoes. "You know they say that a man's cock's jus' half as long as his feet; an' I was jus' a thinking. Or maybe you jus' wear them long shoes to make women think you're a better man than you are!"

They'd laughed together, manly, conspiratorially, although Fox was embarrassed that the lady of the house stood nearby and possibly heard.

Carrying the watch package in one hand, Fox turned onto Wetmore Avenue and let the friendly wood cottages point him down the backstretch to home.

When he was inside the bright, comfortable house, he uncovered the watch and inspected it a moment, gleaming brightly under the artificial light. Then he carefully placed it back and wrapped the box in brown postal paper. With deliberate handwriting he addressed the package: Gracie Emmett, 509 Third Avenue, #4, Seattle.

Gracie was gone from Everett.

Happy New Year Kid!

Well, dear Gracie, how are you getting along?

Up here things go on much as usual, only worse. Upstairs there's been all kinds of illness—the other day the ambulance took a gal from #3—she suddenly became paralyzed from the shoulders on down—which gave a hell of a shock to the guy (her husband or whatever it was) who had just been having his fun with her. I went up there later to see about having the bed made up for another party who wanted a place to shack up. The bed was a mess—bloody sheets & pillow cases: guess she had started to bleed at both ends at once! The hotel called Dr. Beatty; when he came up & looked at this gal he shrugged his shoulders, said "Oh, she's just a little nervous, she'll be all right presently." Finally Doc Farrel was contacted, and when he came up & gave her one look he wanted to know why in hell he hadn't been called before. I guess the dame is in a damned bad mess—may be an invalid for a long time.

Poor Walt is on the shelf again—someone said he's got pneumonia—came down with it just yesterday. Helen told me last night he'd been put on a strictly liquid diet. I said yes, that's what he & I had been on a couple nights ago when I was up in his room for a few minutes. On a diet strictly liquor rather—someone had presented him with a bottle of Portuguese brandy & around 5 a.m. he buzzed me & I went up, thinking perhaps he was sick or something. But he simply wanted to drink with me to the Christmas just passed & the New Year soon to come. So we drank to the future, whatever it would bring. And then he had to go "pop" and get sick, poor old boy.

What the future, this bright New Year, will bring us all the devil only knows. To many I know damned well, to many a poor sailor and soldier out there somewhere it will bring death or bodies torn to bleeding stumps, horrible things to someday come back to mothers, wives or gals they'd left behind full of kisses and sweet goodbye's. I often think of this when I see them talking and laughing on street corners, or in the lobby of the hotel. The effect on parents, wives, when they receive one of those stark notices from the War Department announcing that so-and-so has been killed in action, the effect is generally the same, white faces, women's tears and hysteria, a sort of crumpling up of the body suddenly in many instances.

This Christmas Eve was very quiet at the hotel, and I didn't do much celebrating otherwise either. Just not in the mood, somehow or other. Not doing anything New Years either.

Well Gracie Gal, this letter is somehow not a very damned cheerful one I'm afraid—it's sort of morbid in spirit, just like I feel tonight. Wish you were here and we could toss off a pint just for fun. "Be drunken always," said a wise philosopher. But what would he do if he were like me and only got sick? At least, Gracie, you're lucky you can really get drunk, and forget the cares of this lousy world we're condemned to live in, for a time anyway.

Glad you like the little watch. But the initials are missing, Gracie, because they couldn't promise such work completed before Christmas.

And so this letter comes to an end. More another day. I hope you're getting better kid,—hope indeed that you're alright again.

Mother comes in the room to remind me to say "better days to come, Grace & Happy New Year to you." And I say the same thing Gracie Gal, and may that hold you until my next letter.—Ed Fox, December 1943

8

Revenge in small doses

*H**ello Dad, Mother and all: I'm still here in Japan and feeling as well as can be expected. I received your radiogram recently, it told me all I wish to know namely that everyone was well. Everything is better for us with the coming of summer months. There is little else to say except I hope to be with you before long. With all my love, Jack*

Scarce letters sent home held lies; living, dying, all of it.

Jack wavered between light and dark for several weeks and could've slipped over easily enough, cremated ashes in a flimsy pine box. His temperature soared dangerously high. He was too weak to eat and too stubborn not to.

"Don't you die on me," Hanson said over and again, offering him pellets of rice that Jack mouthed like an old man and swallowed dry.

Light and dark, day and night, death and release.

A few feet away, cocooned on another of those endless wooden bays in that same cold warehouse, Sergeant Odas Greer was gritty as ever. Now and again a sliver of Japanese gunmetal worked its way out from deep in his muscles and he plucked it out when it broke skin. Just holding on, the sergeant told himself as if some part of him needed reminding. The days blurred into one anonymous gray sameness, a captive's markings on the calendar in his head.

Listen, it was like this: The sound of coughing. Of low talking, when there was such energy. The rubbing of wind against the warehouse siding.

The crunch of gravel on parade grounds. The yellow stare of overhead lights. The smell of unclean skin. The nighttime gnawing of rats on mess kit tins.

That's what it was and that's why it was all the same, day after day.

Sergeant Greer began a secret diary. To be caught keeping score like that invited severe beatings, possibly death, but he kept at it anyway, scribbling defiantly in his small, hidden book.

That was at night on his cramped little sleeping bay. Daytime, like everyone else in the Yokohama labor camp, he toiled alongside Japanese civilians at the Mitsubishi shipyard. Forcing war prisoners into slave labor violated the codes of conduct agreed upon at the International Red Cross Geneva convention of 1929, but Japan never ratified the codes and felt unbound by such rules. They'd treat their captives however they pleased.

And so every morning, fueled by a cup of fish soup and a few mouthfuls of hot plain rice, the men marched five abreast, 500 strong, from the prison yard.

The first mile took them across a wood bridge and down dark, sleepy streets of scrunched-in Asian storefronts. In the beginning Japanese children gaped openly at the walking white scarecrows, but in time they became part of the city's landscape, their dead stares fading off down the street.

Onward they marched past storefronts of Kanji lettering and tired bicycles, and past the bathhouse window where steam curled out on frosty mornings. The thought of sinking into one of those tubs and soaking away the months of grime and ache was luxurious beyond anything imaginable. And the guards needn't have been so annoyed one morning when two women in bright kimonos ducked before the prisoners into the bathhouse. The young hollow-cheeked POWs were too weak for any stirring in their loins.

Onward they marched, five abreast, 500 strong, the men on the outer rows occasionally stooping like stewbums to fetch a discarded cigarette butt. Diarrhea ran down pantlegs, dripping into the heels of unlaced shoes.

At one mile, near the Yokohama train station, the prisoners turned from the eye of Mount Fuji, which broke over the horizon like a strange Buddha god, and entered the city's industrial waterfront. The Mitsubishi shipyard was geometry oversized. Timbered ways launched ship after ship, and nearly a dozen huge steel cranes on rail tracks cast long spindly shadows across the docks. The place buzzed with wartime fever. The clanking of metal being cut, shaped, and riveted into giant ship's hulls permeated across the yards, as did the acrid smell of machinery.

Here the prisoners broke ranks and joined the mob of civilians working as methodically and silently as ants in a colony.

Every morning, regular as the Army, Greer took his broom and dustpan and began sweeping piles of metal filings from under noisy machinist benches. All around him prisoners moved uncomfortably beneath Kanji work signs, their bony arms flapping inside loose-sleeved Mitsubishi coats.

They were ordinary men from the vast farmlands and cities of America, who found their revenge in small doses. Sabotage was anywhere that a man who'd left a friend for dead on the roads of Bataan discovered a deserted ship-yard shaft or a darkened waterfront passage. Prisoners tossed canfuls of oil or various metal debris into engine parts. They drove nails through electrical conduits, dropped handfuls of nuts and bolts into turbines, or scattered pea gravel in pipes.

Months later, the heavy bearings on new Japanese warships mysteriously burned out. Steam turbines on trial runs exploded for no reason. POWs watched new ships sail out of Tokyo Bay and innocently awaited their limp return.

All across the Greater East Asia Co-Prosperity Sphere under the blood-shot eye of the Japanese rising sun, Allied prisoners plotted revenge. In the Philippines, sun-leathered prisoners poured sand down the oil ports of trucks. In the zinc mines of the Japanese mainland, POWs casually gathered around train car wheels. With the guards distracted, quick clever hands opened the axle's stuffing box, pulled out the batting, tossed in handfuls of sand, and closed it back up. Before long the procedure was timed to perfection.

In those same mines, at the end of each day, other prisoners gathered handfuls of metal drill filings and rolled them into their trouser cuffs. Back in camp they shook the metal onto sheets of newspaper. The next morning another gang smuggled those shavings into the maintenance shed and stirred them in cans of grease. Before long, jackhammers all over the mine sputtered and died.

Even so, the Japanese guards refused to concede that their lazy, slow-witted prisoners were capable of such tricks.

Whenever the opportunity arose, Greer casually gathered up dustpans of steel shavings and drifted toward the nearest metal hatch. Acting as disinterested as possible, he nimbly unlatched the cover and dumped in his load. One such hatch protected a shaft containing three giant bearings leading to the propeller of a ship.

Take that, he muttered to himself. That night in his sleeping bay he retrieved his stubby pencil, snuggled into his blankets, and wrote: "They caught two fellows and they disappeared, don't know where they went."

Right left, right left, just like boot camp, his automatic footsteps kept time with the others, his mind blank, his body consumed by stabs of hunger. But somewhere between the guardhouse and gate, he snapped to alert when the tired line suddenly ground to a stop. Before he knew it a sentry was running up to his face. Shit. This was bad. Exposed like this, there was nowhere to hide.

"Pitchee," Greer said, motioning to his mouth. Greer was small, the size of most Japanese guards, and he hoped that admitting his transgression would ease the inevitable. He knew that being singled out never was good. Worse yet, it wasn't the first time he'd been caught chewing the tasteless black tar that was spread between the planking of Mitsubishi ships.

"Pitchee Domi Nada."

The prisoners sometimes grabbed a dab of it to chew, its soothing texture giving their teeth and gums the illusion of food.

He reached inside his mouth and handed the wad of black tar to the guard, who examined the contraband as if it were an affront to the Emperor. The first offense for chewing pitch was a face slapping. Next came a beating. This was Greer's third offense.

Shortly after their capture, prisoners had discovered that punishment rolled downhill. If a superior struck a Japanese soldier, that soldier skulked about until he found someone lower in rank. War prisoners, being the lowest of human life, scrapped out an existence at the bottom of all hills, and thus were fair game for any sort of unprovoked beatings. It was best, therefore, to fade into the background, numbers without names, part of the anonymous stubble-haired, white-skinned herd. Breaking that basic law of anonymity brought consequences you just didn't want to think about. By then it was too late anyway.

While the rest of the prisoners continued into the barracks, Greer remained outside on the parade ground near the small wooden guardhouse. A breeze from the bay blew the smell of seaweed over him. Soon it would be winter again, the nights stretching out long and rainy, not unlike those back home. He didn't consider home much anymore, no one did. It was too far-gone and too long ago—too removed from the immediate problems of staying alive in this hostile land.

Greer's stomach grumbled for food and he resented dinner passing him by, his small portion spread among other prisoners. They could probably see him through the barracks warehouse window, standing on the washed-out gravel awaiting judgement.

Eventually the sun dipped beneath Yokohama's skyline and a soldier emerged from the guardhouse carrying a swab of black pitch in his white-gloved hand. He held it out from him as if it were excrement.

The guards were never hungry. Their arms and legs and chests filled their official green uniforms. Their faces were fleshed out and healthy, not emaciated and sallow like Greer's. They always had the strength to punch or poke or practice their martial arts on defenseless prisoners they knew couldn't fight back.

The worst of the guards were secretly given nicknames: "White Angel," big and mean; "Buddha," a snake in the body of a monk; "Punchy," who earned his name for his straight-ahead blows.

Greer chewed the soft tar while the guard handed him two one-gallon wood buckets filled with water. He was told to hold them out at arm's length. The guard reached into Greer's mouth, roughly extracting the black ball of tar before shoving it on the tip of his nose. He resembled a clown in his thin Mitsubishi coat; head shaved, buckets out, and the black tar drooping off his nose. To resist such humiliation, however, invited even greater consequences, a severe beating at the least. It meant nothing to them.

No, the smart move was to take it and live, to scribble again in the secret diary, and hope for a liberation that didn't include your ashes poured inside one of those pine boxes stacked in the warehouse where everyone could see.

Already Greer's arms ached. The smirking guard waited. The minutes on his wristwatch ticked by. Before long, one of the wood buckets fell to the gravel. The guard leapt for it and Greer felt the shock of cold water splashing over his head, freezing down his collar and neck. His cold shirt stuck to his back.

Now he held the second bucket before him with both hands. But even then it grew too heavy. When he could hold it no longer, that bucket, too, tumbled to the gravel.

Again the guard sprang forward and tossed water over him. They were probably laughing inside the guardhouse.

It was evening now and the chill seeped through Greer's skin until his muscles and bones seemed to freeze in place. He trembled from a cold deep within, a heartless, cruel cold.

When the prisoners in the warehouse barracks rose the next morning and looked out toward the callused eye of Mount Fuji, there was Greer still standing on the gravel parade ground.

Only then was he was allowed to return to the warehouse in time for his breakfast of rice and lukewarm soup.

After that he lined up with the prisoners marching five abreast, 500 strong, past the storefronts and the bathhouse to the Mitsubishi shipyards, where he gathered up his broom and dustpan for another day of work.

Lots of them figured well, so what's the use of living? Of course I tried everything I could to keep living. Consider the number of men who didn't make it, who died. Whatever had to come I was gonna' make it.—Odas Greer

From wall to wall across the great stretch of the open Yokohama warehouse, prisoners just returned from a day of hard labor sat on their wood bays in quiet expectation.

"Ooo dahlers!" called the Dutch Army prisoners, who were captured in the East Indies. Their sandpaper voices told the food haulers to pick up dinner, 20 men per bucket of rice.

Jack smelled the rice and soup before it arrived, hand carried from the nearby kitchen in steaming wood buckets. His mouth watered.

Issuing rice was the toughest prison camp job and it rotated among the POWs. Fists flew if the serving cup was packed too tight or too loose—it had to be the same for everyone. They were starving animals circling a half-eaten carcass.

Some scarfed their rice where they stood; others stared at the kit in their hands, as if eating slow would make those tiny white grains multiply.

Jack grabbed his share, satisfied he hadn't been cheated, and climbed the ladder to his bay to eat in privacy. He'd slowly recovered from the sickness that stole his strength when he first arrived in Yokohama. Day after day he grew stronger, until in his mind he knew there was nothing they could do to even the score. Not with the memory of three Japanese bodies twitching in the Corregidor sun.

Supper was his only moment of solace in a long day. Leftovers, called taps, were distributed evenly down the line, fair and square, although most nights there were none.

Afterwards, their rations licked clean, the hungry prisoners entertained themselves with elaborate recipes, outscoring one another with the richness of their dreams. Jack listened in.

"The first thing I'm gonna' do when I get outta here," their sentences would begin before soaring off into a fantasy land where steaks were the size of catcher's mitts, loaves of bread as big and white as church doors. They'd wrestle with slabs of yellow butter and coffee, real coffee, and enough ice cream to fill a washtub. Crowning the ice cream were fresh, sweet strawberries. After dinner a waiter wearing a spotless white coat would appear with a fat nickel stogie. The thought of cigar smoke curling up their faces after such a glorious feast kept them occupied for a moment—before the rice emptiness returned to bellies filled only with disappointment.

While some dreamt of food, others played poker. They were loud, serious games, for cigarettes were the gamble and tobacco a volatile market. Pockets of men huddled together around sleeping bays scrutinizing their homemade cards, considering the odds. Others, too poor or too careful to join in, watched over their shoulders.

A prisoner with a bad habit might exchange a meal or two for cigarettes, issued once a month. Those determined to outright kill themselves traded away so much rice that they literally smoked themselves to death.

Like cigarettes, rice was its own currency. Prisoners might exchange a half ration of food one day for the promise of a full one later. A prisoner with no willpower might find himself drowning in a debt of rice and that's when it helped to have friends.

Johannsen, who'd regained his strength under the nurturing of Hanson and Jack, grew dangerously impulsive. At one stretch he agreed to surrender more than a week's worth of rations for the immediacy of extra food. For several days in a row, he took his overflowing kit back to his bay and greedily gobbled down the rice, its warmth barely touching the great hunger inside.

One evening at supper, several scruffy looking prisoners appeared around Johannsen, one by one demanding their rice.

"What rice?" he asked weakly.

"The rice you owe us."

Hanson and Jack looked up from their meal and quickly moved between them. Johannsen's dogfaced expression said it all. Somehow, he admitted to Jack, it'd slipped out of control until now he'd starve to death if forced to re-pay what he owed. Jack eyed the hungry prisoners. They were in no mood to forgive. They wanted their rice.

There was nothing to do but declare Johannsen bankrupt. Either that or watch him die.

Those he'd stiffed would just have to accept that they'd made a bum trans-action, and if they didn't like it they could wade through the fists of Hanson and Jack to get at him.

The prisoners sized it up and decided it wasn't worth it. They turned away, sullenly retreating to their side of the warehouse. Such undercurrents of resentment over food and tobacco coursed through the barracks. Some prisoners, driven to thievery, stole anything they could lay their hands on, which wasn't much. Food was particularly valuable and any excess required close guarding or fast eating.

Jack knew how it felt to be stiffed. Once, early on, Johannsen owed him some rice. It wasn't much, but the thought of a little extra chow kept him pleasantly occupied one day in the cold Mitsubishi shipyards. Later, at dinnertime he came to collect.

"Joe, where's that ration you owe me?"

Johannsen looked away.

"I already ate it," he mumbled softly.

It was rainy that evening, with low clouds sweeping across the waterfront, but in a spark of anger Jack dragged his friend outside. Despite the rain, a group of prisoners soon gathered in the parade ground to watch. Those expecting blood were disappointed.

The combatants stood flat-footed in the gravelly mud, swinging wildly from somewhere around their knees and connecting only with soggy air. Once Jack swung with a mighty heave and tumbled over, muddying his clothes. He rose slowly on one knee, panting to catch his breath. Then it was Johannsen's turn to fall. Before long the anger inside Jack fizzled.

Filling its place was the realization that here in this Yokohama prison camp his youth had been stolen from him, dried up and blown away like an autumn leaf. He no more had the energy to quarterback his high school team than he could escape this hell. He couldn't even finish a miserable fight.

When you're young and come upon a fence in a meadow of wild flowers and tall grass, you leap over without a second thought. Now and maybe forever forward, Jack knew he would walk a long way just to find an opening in that fence. He fought like an old man. He felt like an old man. It frightened him. He looked at Johannsen beside him, panting wildly and covered in mud. Two pathetic shitbums scrapping over a couple grains of rice.

Jack had just turned 21.

Dear Folks, I am safe and well here in camp. I came thru without injury. We get plenty of exercise. Xmas we received a package from the Red Cross. I hope everyone there is in good health. I will write again soon. Love, Jack

Lies, all of it. Lies.

Jack heaved his body against a black barrel of cooking oil lined up beside an endless sea of others on the Mitsubishi dock. It was a bitter winter morning and he grunted from the effort, hugging his arms about his ribby chest.

Safe and well. He wrote what he had to, what he knew the Japanese censors would allow. Anyway, what was he going to write, that the years of hunger, boredom, disappointment, and acceptance now creased the face of every captive he knew? That thousands of them had died, many of them fellow Marines, and who knew how many more would follow?

I came thru without injury. No use worrying the folks back home any more than they already were.

Before long, Jack finished lugging the barrel from the dock to a growing pile in the hard-packed sand near the water. A cold breeze blew off the bay and seemed to gather strength as it whistled through the mid-sized freighters and gray Japanese warships. It was always cold on the waterfront, always that sharp breeze as constant in his face as hunger in his belly.

Dai Toa Senso, the great war, was not unfolding the way the Japanese military had promised its people. America had found its strength and now fought tantalizingly close to Japan, leapfrogging the endless Pacific Ocean islands and scoring bloody victories on tropical beachfronts. After the initial success at Pearl Harbor, in the East Indies, and the Philippines, the war was extracting a terrible price on the Japanese homeland.

The Allied prisoners followed the war as best they could through discarded newspapers lying about the shipyard. Not that they understood the confusing Kanji words and squiggles. But common sense and Pacific geography told them that when the papers printed maps of islands that were increasingly closer to Japan—the Solomons, Gilberts, Marshalls, and Saipan—the Americans weren't far behind.

Cooking oil barrels by the hundreds were stacked on the Mitsubishi dock that stretched on wood pilings into the bay. Moving them to the beach would take several days, perhaps weeks, but Jack had nothing but time and in its own way the job was satisfying. After a few trips from the dock to the sand, the exertion warmed him. He liked the feel of the heavy oil barrels.

The 997 and red stripe sewn into his prison coat seemed to shine through the foggy low clouds. Wrapped tight around his stomach was an eight-inch wide strip of wool blanket he called a bellyband. After more than two years in the Yokohama warehouse, the prisoners learned that a warm belly kept chills from spreading.

Quite without warning that morning he noticed a movement in the sand. There it was again. Two Japanese girls appeared to be digging near one of the barrels. They hadn't seen him. He stopped, transformed by the moment. He guessed they were about 12 years old. They could've been girls anywhere, lost in play along a busy industrial waterfront. But it was early morning, and cold, and this was war.

He might've stood there longer just staring, but then one of the girls looked up.

He must have appeared huge to them, a pale starving beast with blue sunken eyes, the red stripe on his chest burning like some bloody talisman. The Japanese civilians had been warned about the Americans; they were cannibals, they were freaks. They were the enemy.

The girls' hands shook in fright. Jack thought they must've come from a factory complex just beyond a fence near the shipyard. He approached down the dock, calming them with a few words of broken Japanese.

He discovered they were after cooking oil that stained the sand around a barrel. By 1944, food and oil shortages in Japan had become acute. That which was available fueled the war and starved the civilians.

Jack took the girl's small cans to a leaky barrel hidden in a pile. The barrel had cracked in transport and now slowly dripped its precious cargo. He filled the two small containers and handed them to the girls, who watched breathlessly. They bowed.

Jack pointed to a place near the fence where the girls were to leave their cans next morning. They bowed again and disappeared.

When he arrived at the dock the following day, Jack found the two cans hidden where he had instructed. He filled them with oil and left them there. The next morning the empty cans appeared again, only inside this time were two soft children's cookies.

The exchange lasted every morning for a couple weeks until the oil ran out. Jack never saw his young friends again. If he could've sat and talked to them freely, he might have tried explaining why, even while living in that awful camp, he didn't hate their people. Maybe he would've told them about

Corregidor, how he was a combat soldier who shot and killed, but not from any personal malice, how he was surprised mainly just to be alive. There's nothing anyone can do to even the score, he might have told them. Maybe they would've understood as children sometimes do.

As it was, Jack never even learned their names.

Dear folks, I hope this finds you in good health. I am Okay. Hanson and I are still together. Not many boot camp friends left. Jack

9

The voice of madness
(hell ship, 1944)

*T*HE EARTHEN WALLS OF BILIBID PRISON seemed especially dark and mean, holding back centuries of despair. It was more real than that for Henry Chamberlain, of course, who'd never fully understood his captors' blind hatred behind those walls two years earlier. Not then, not now. But the cigar burns on his forearms and the nauseating reminder of his own scorched flesh was a testament to it. What kind of minds brokered such anger?

Now he was back inside Bilibid. Like before it was only a stopover, a jumping off point from Manila in the Philippines to a nightmare somewhere else.

It began October 1, 1944, when he and a thousand others mulishly milled about the prison yard while impatient guards goaded them into formation. Eventually they marched out the gated grounds, down shady tree-lined Quezon Boulevard, and toward Manila Bay where fresh breezes from the South China Sea fanned the city.

After breathing moldy prison air, the breeze was welcome on his tanned face. So too was the warm sunshine. To his left and right and back several deep on Quezon Boulevard, sympathetic Filipinos lined up to watch. When his eyes drifted from brown face to brown face, he occasionally saw surreptitious fingers spread into a V for victory and "The Star Spangled Banner" came whistling out from somewhere in the crowd. A tendril of hope had settled over Japanese-occupied Manila.

A few days earlier, Henry had been unloading cargo from a Japanese freighter when the sound of engines caused him to look up. He shielded his eyes from the sun and tried to make out the markings on the aircraft silhouetted against the endless blue sky. He watched in a trance. One by one they peeled off and dove towards him. Now he could see they were American planes with plain white stars on the wings. Such a beautiful sight. The surprised guards screamed at the prisoners, who seemed rooted to the dock, unable to move. *American planes, imagine that!* The flustered guards dove for cover among piles of wooden supply boxes stacked up on the busy waterfront. How odd, Henry thought, the air raid sirens never sounded.

Bombs exploded around him, sizzling to earth, scorching the anchored Japanese ships and directing plumes of white spray onto the dock until he was drenched. Clouds of oily black smoke smudged the sky. Yet, he was transfixed.

"They're back," Henry shouted above the din, a goofy grin plastered to his face. "They're back."

Several ships were sinking; others had been hit as well and bled tarry smoke. But still he was unafraid, as if Yankee armament could distinguish between enemy and friend.

Now, much too late, the air raid siren bleated a mournful wail. Anti-aircraft guns positioned around the harbor boomed a response, but the flak burst far short of the retreating American warplanes that climbed back into the sky in tight formation before disappearing, the grind of their engines lost in the distance.

There were only minor wounds among the scraggly prisoners who cheered as if at a baseball game.

"They're back," Henry said again, this time to convince himself. "Now it's our turn."

He marched by on Quezon Boulevard now, catching faint traces of "The Star Spangled Banner" floating out from the crowd. Henry seemed to gather strength. Certainly the bombing from a few days earlier restored his hope in liberation. What a comical picture he would present to the Americans when they did arrive. He weighed no more than 80 pounds on legs so thin they seemed lost inside his patched khaki shorts. The sleeves of his shirt were sacrificed long ago. His skin was leathery from years in the tropical sun and it could've belonged to a middle-aged man. His sockless feet were still wrapped inside homemade wooden clogs that clacked awkwardly down the street, but little matter, the Americans soon would return to Manila.

The formation of prisoners continued down Quezon until it arrived at the docks, and then alongside a rusty ship riding high in the water. It was a pitiful old collier with a Red Cross painted on its stack. The line stopped. Henry fought off a moment of rising panic. Why stop before this wretched vessel? Keep moving, keep moving!

But before there was time to give it more thought, they counted off, and then once more, as the guards prodded the prisoners onto the gangplank of the *Haro Maru*. So this was it, the nightmare he'd heard of, the voyage he'd every reason to dread. And just when it seemed his luck was changing.

Henry gulped one last desperate breath of fresh warm air and soaked up the sunshine. He glanced back at Manila's exotic palm trees and the friendly natives living in houses on crooked streets. Then he felt the hard butt of a rifle. The spirit those American planes had provided just days earlier sank within him.

By 1944, when Henry boarded the *Haro Maru*, scores of American submarines roamed the lonely Pacific, picking off Japanese freighters and warships venturing out to supply and defend the Greater East Asia Co-Prosperity Sphere.

In one month alone that year, the Americans torpedoed more than 300,000 tons of Japanese shipping to the ocean floor. The Japanese noose now tightened around the POWs still under guard in the Philippines. Most prisoners took turns, like Henry, marching single file onto unmarked freighters bound for the Japanese mainland, 2,000 miles away. American torpedoes didn't distinguish between Japanese supply ships and those with holds stuffed with Allied prisoners. It was all dirty luck; you died quick from your own Navy's torpedoes or you starved slow from disease and a diet of rice.

At night the Japanese convoys sailed without lights out into Luzon Strait and on toward Formosa over the endless black ocean, with American submarine wolf packs nipping at their heels.

Sitting knee to back in the hopeless squalor of those freighter's cargo holds were the toughest of the tough—survivors of the Bataan Death March and the siege of Corregidor and more than two years of brutal captivity and constant jabs at their spirit. They were a decimated lot, about used up as slave labor. Perhaps now they had another purpose. The ugly rumor spreading among the prisoners inside those hell ships was that they were about to become hostages for the coming American invasion of Japan, as now seemed certain—human slaves, and now human bait.

Henry and the others went into the *Haro Maru* that sunny morning, one after another, vermin into an underground nest. In the ship's belly, 1,000 men were divided, 500 per hold—half to fight their madness in a small metal chamber filled with sharp dirty coal, the others in a scummy enclosure littered with stale horse droppings.

Henry sank down the crusty steel ladder, each step taking him further from the sunlight and into a stifling place, where he scratched for a spot atop shards of coal. A shaft of light from the overhead hatch burned into the filthy black air. Beyond the dust was darkness: humid, moist, and suffocating. A physician among them carried a clinical thermometer and before long it topped out at 108 degrees. It grew hotter as the day advanced and more men stumbled in, each stirring up coal dust that coated their throats and lungs until each breath spewed up rusty mucous chunks.

Terror rose about them and they swallowed it back, although it floated ever closer to the surface of their thoughts. Henry clutched his canteen, mess kit, and his grandfather's straight razor. Always there was that razor, his last connection to the sanity of home. He clung to it like life itself.

That afternoon the ship ventured out a few hundred yards into Manila Bay, where it dropped anchor and sat for two days, turning slowly and imperceptibly with the tides. After that it would join a flotilla of 38 other ships bound for Japan.

Sometime during that first night, while the prisoners rustled miserably against one another, the cross on the ship's stack was painted over. Even at night the air was thick and hot, permeated with the smell of sweat and human waste and the frightful sound of men moaning. The next 39 days were about to unravel in disconnected images that made little sense even when dissected later.

The slapping ocean waves seemed random; back and forth, side to side; panic and then not. The creaking ship reminded Henry of a rusty old tub. Buckets used for toilets hung down from the ceiling and pendulumed with the ocean's swells, clapping the ship's sides and spilling onto prisoners below. Dysentery spread. Prisoners shat themselves. Odd smells ripened in the unbearable heat, spoiling as if rotting flesh. Flies appeared in the brown coal air and multiplied into a pestilence. The prisoners hovered on the very edge of insanity, venturing a few steps over and then retreating back, weak and scared.

Henry had an idea. With the help of another prisoner, he cut a rope into pieces and cinched both ends of his Army blanket. He tied the ends to holes in the steel stanchions running up the inside of the ship's hold. Before long he had a hammock, rising a few feet off the sharp, dirty coal. Others followed. Soon there was more room for those left on the pile below.

Henry drifted in and out, his hammock gently rocking in rhythm with the *Haro Maru*. Small rivulets of moisture beaded up on the ship's side. He found a dirty cloth, wiped the sweat off the metal, and eagerly squeezed the liquid into his mouth. The droplets only teased. Thirst was everywhere and, when he breathed, the stale air clutched at his dry throat.

Then he was rocking again, drifting in and out, the gentle clacking of buckets overhead keeping time with the waves.

There was a girl from Spokane he was determined to marry. But now what was there? What of the family they could've had, coffee with breakfast in a cool shady summerhouse? Where was that now?

A prisoner died. There was no service, no obituary or chaplain's grace. His corpse was tied to a rope and up it swung, twisting and thumping like those overflowing buckets of shit, until it disappeared from sight. A burial detail followed up the ladder, untied the body, and dropped it overboard.

Thirty-nine prisoners would perish aboard the *Haro Maru*, averaging one a day, for those keeping score. When one of them was gently pushed overboard, the gassy body floated rather than sunk, bouncing off the ship until it spun free and into the path of a trailing destroyer. The body flummoxed against the destroyer's steel hull again and again, until it was sucked into the viscously turning screws. Sickened by the sight, a prisoner mouthed a silent prayer before a guard poked him with a rifle and he scurried below.

It's impossible to describe to someone who's never been in that situation but you develop a mindset, you kind of turn everything off except for what you're doing right now. You become a blank. Most of the time lapsed into a state of almost nothing. Almost like going into a non-dream. It's blank, inactive, a dream state, for days on end.—Henry Chamberlain

Ping. Henry listened for the sonar wave and rose slightly on his hammock. There it was again. Ping. The message grew against the steel ship and seemed to echo inside the hold. Ping, ping.

Somewhere down there in the freezing depths, an American submarine stalked them. He felt the Japanese convoy zigzag over the endless ocean, trying to outmaneuver the inevitable. But they'd been seen and now an American submarine shadowed them. The Japanese guards slapped wood planks over the holds, covered them with canvas tarps, and winched down steel cable. Sealed now inside their coffin, there was nothing to do but wait for a torpedo to end it.

A chaplain led the ashen-faced men in prayer. Afterwards it was deathly quiet. Ping. The sound wave bounced off the ship again. Death was that close, just outside the sweaty steel hull that held back the force of the ocean itself. Depth charges from the Japanese flotilla exploded underwater, one after another. From his hammock, Henry felt the freighter rock from the concussion waves. A wild-eyed Navy petty officer, his hands grasping a canteen, suddenly broke the silence. Clamb! Clamb!—his canteen striking the hull again and again, creating a weird metallic rhythm. The harsh pounding reverberated through the hold and seemed to focus into short out-of-control bursts: Clamb! Clamb!

"Come get us you sons' a bitches, come get us," the Navy man screamed. Others tried to hold him back, but he screamed louder and fought against their grasp. "Come get us."

If we're gonna take a hit, make it a good clean one, Henry thought. *End it. Hurry up, hurry up, get it over with.*

He didn't want to be alive when the freighter went down. He didn't want to fight off a thousand desperate prisoners clawing for escape through the ragged hole he knew a torpedo would make. He didn't want to taste the final fear in his throat as cold seawater rushed in and lifted weightless men up and up, until they floated along with the black chunks of coal in the dark metal coffin, gasping and suffocating as water flooded their lungs.

Henry heard a torpedo explosion, and then another outside somewhere, and imagined a merchant ship burning on the water, terrified Japanese sailors swimming through the bright, oily flames.

As a boy, Henry once sold ice cream cups and frozen candy bars from an insulated box tied to the handlebars of his bicycle. On summer days he'd dodge the autos that ground past him on dusty roads. He'd pedal faster, out to where the airport workers stood in the hot sun under a cloudless sky. Some wandered over to his bicycle, flipping nickels through the air, which he'd catch with practiced hands. When he reached inside the box, steam from the dry ice melted in the summer heat.

When his case was empty and his pocket full of nickels, he'd pedal over to a hangar where a man waited, moving stiffly around his cloth-covered biplane. As Henry walked his bike into the shade of the hangar, the man looked up and grunted hello. Before long, they were taxiing down a runway, the hot Omaha afternoon rushing through Henry's hair, the biplane's engine roaring in his ears. Up they climbed over the city and past the farmers' cornfields that from the air were neat, civilized rows, the way all cornfields should be, their pleated geometry taming the great Midwest plain. On they flew until the fields beneath them turned to plain, barren earth stretching to where the horizon met the sky.

The pilot had been wounded in World War I and one leg was shorter than the other, so he walked unevenly, as if catching himself with every step. He'd rigged blocks on the pedals of his plane to bring them up to his short leg. On the ground he was crippled, but in the air he was an acrobat. They flew graceful arcs over the prairie below. When they spotted a coyote loping through the sagebrush, he dropped the plane low, skimming across the baked earth until it seemed as if he could smell fear in the animal's breath. Henry took aim and the shotgun in his hands exploded. They'd circle back, while Henry dropped a paper sack filled with flour. A pack of coyote carcasses might yield four or five white flour marks on the prairie floor. Later they'd land the biplane near the bodies. The man bent over, cut through the cartilage of an ear, and dropped it in a sack, each ear worth 50 cents bounty.

When it rained, the pilot's war-busted knee and hip ached. Sometimes, when the pain was too much, he'd hit the bottle hard. He'd fly crazy then, pulling suicidal stunts. Once he flew towards a bridge spanning the Missouri River. The airplane cut underneath near the slow moving water and looped over the top, missing the feathery span by inches and then down underneath again, the airplane's roar bouncing off the river's muddy banks. It was better than legs.

There was another man in town with a thick black beard whose jaw had been blown off in the Great War. Only guttural sounds came from his disfigured face. He was a common laborer, a man who took any kind of job to survive. He had his own booth at a small neighborhood restaurant. Around the booth was a curtain, which the waitress closed when she placed a bowl of pureed food before him. When the meal arrived and the curtain closed, he'd pull open his gullet hole and spooned in a load of the gluey mess. He rubbed his throat until the liquid slopped far enough down to swallow, parts of it dribbling onto strands of his beard. Water from a glass helped clear it away.

Other war veterans buried their scars deeper inside. Around the Fourth of July each year, they hid in cornfields safe from the booming fireworks that stirred up memories best left buried.

The screams were haunting, piercing through the coal dust. They died around him of dysentery, thirst, and, of course, starvation. Beriberi raced through their feet until the slightest bump on the sharp coal shot through them. Prisoners soiled themselves. Tempers flared. Fights erupted.

Madness waited, biding its time, then seeped into their brains until it took hold, growing and spreading. Then it was everywhere, a thick chilling shriek that gathered momentum, an out-of-control disease. Men sat beside each other and howled like animals. Henry couldn't erase the sound from his mind. "We're dead! We're deaaaaaad!"

More laughter, screaming out of insanity itself. You could see it and feel it coming at you like distant headlights in the night.

"We're deaaaaad!"

"Shuddup!"

"We're deaaad!"

"Damn your soul!"

Beat them until they stop, beat them. Kill if you have to, just shut them up. Kill them, kill them!

But the howling continued, making you crazy too, lying on your filthy blanket hammock, rolling with every wave of the mocking ocean. There was no law. Kill it. There was no authority, no courts, no discipline. Kill it, kill it, kill it all. It was like being drunk, blackout drunk, so when you awoke you didn't know what you'd done or where you'd been.

"He stole my water. He stole my fucking water."

It was beyond anything he knew, a brushfire spreading fast. Henry listened as a prisoner accused another of stealing his water canteen. Before anyone could stop him, the prisoner grabbed the canteen back and the two skeletons wrestled on a dirty pile of coal.

Henry watched as the prisoner suddenly knelt over the panting thief, using the canteen to batter his head. No one could've stopped it. The thief was silent then, with cold glassy eyes. Later that night he died.

10

Streets paved with options
(Seattle, 1944)

W HEN THE SMALLISH PACKAGE with the careful handwriting arrived, Gracie glanced at the return address and then tore at the simple brown wrapping.

As her eyes broke over the typewritten sentences, a raw ache surely rose and filled the drab room. Only poor, untethered people lived in such hotels with faint odors of unforgiven sin.

Along with the letter was a box and inside lay a pink gold Parker's Lady wristwatch. Gracie turned it over in her hands. There was no inscription on the back, nothing to connect her with Everett or the man who sent it. Yet, when she slipped it over her wrist, the fit was perfect.

Dear Ed, Just received your little watch honey it sure is a cute little thing, I am crazy about it. I don't know how to thank you for it. I was sure surprised. —Gracie

She'd seen enough to know she couldn't stay, even if it meant leaving Ed with his books and bow ties and who wouldn't ever desert Everett, much less in the company of someone like her.

The thought of him loading thousands of his precious books into heavy wooden trunks and then waving goodbye to his mother and the house on Wetmore Avenue was laughable. It couldn't be discussed.

So Gracie did what she had to and followed those invisible footsteps into the familiar landscape of a cheap Seattle hotel room, 25 miles downsound from the smokestacks of Everett. No regrets. Don't cry for lost Gracie, she with her incurable itch to be postmarked elsewhere.

Gracie was a flapper from the '20s, who'd watched her best years melt away in the '30s and now wanted more than ever to survive the war without advice, friendly or otherwise. And what better place than Seattle, where every corner had choices, every new face possibilities. There was anonymity as well, if that was what you sought—streets paved with options.

Block-long department stores buzzed with shoppers and the mighty shipyards contributed sweat and steel to the war effort.

At night, under the glow of downtown street lights, the Negro soldiers and sailors from bases as far away as Paine Field in Everett and Oak Harbor on Whidbey Island ducked into jazz clubs chipped unnoticed into the brick and concrete storefronts. Sometimes, for a fleeting moment, a hot chord escaped into the street where it was crackling lightning, too searing and primal for passersby to touch.

Seattle could also be an unforgiving city that would suck you in and forget you existed. Watch your backside. But Gracie, being Gracie, walked straight in with her eyes wide open, as they say, an all-business look frozen on her determined face. She could be hard, too. She spoke their language. She'd show them all. As Fox would say, Gracie was a bit of all right.

Then it began to unravel, like before. Like everywhere. Gracie discovered that even in Seattle there were teeth that needed pulling, fevers, ear aches, blood poisoning, overdrinking, and assorted other bruises of body and spirit.

The annoying Northwest rain dripped out of impossibly washed-out skies just as it had in Everett. Instead of endless possibilities, Seattle was filled with unconnected faces that seemed to float up out of the mist and disappear into fog.

"I sure don't care for Seattle but guess I will like it for a while whether I want to or not," she grumbled in a letter to Fox.

Catastrophe waited at her doorstep. Most times she invited it right in. When she needed it most, Gracie lost a warm winter coat. In another of her letters, which were often a scribbled sentence or two on scraps of notepaper, she beseeched Fox for money.

Gracie found a barmaid job, then, like her winter coat, lost it. She went to work at the Holland Coffee Shop, making just enough to cover rent at the Corona Hotel. She lasted exactly four shifts.

"I went dashing in the storeroom after some salt and went head over heels on a case of canned goods, knocked my knee cap out of place so here I am again for a little spell. Just as well of broke the damn thing and had it over with but didn't," she wrote.

One winter night it was so cold a dope fiend upstairs started a fire to keep warm. Eventually the vice squad raided the place and hauled away the crazy woman, whose demented laughter echoed through the lonely halls.

Gracie sent Fox scurrying about Everett after a pair of war-stamp shoes she'd left behind in the care of a drunk named Mickey.

A few weeks later she ordered him on a reconnaissance mission to a number of Hewitt Avenue taverns where she had worked, a month here, a week or two there, in search of her income tax pay stubs. Fox dutifully reported back:

When I went into Dixon's to get your earnings slip, the first thing the boss asked me was, "And how is Grace, anyway? Haven't seen her for a long time; heard she was in Seattle. Got a Christmas card from her, but there was no return on it, or I would have sent her a card too." It was around 4 p.m. and business was only so-so. "Well," said the boss as I took off, "be sure and say Hello to Grace for me."

"Never did get that girl's address," said the man down at the Eagles when I asked for your slip.

The Yukon is a hell of a place to get into—never seems to be open. It isn't the Yukon any more either—name has recently been changed to Joe & Irene's. Quite a few beer spots here have changed hands since you left. The Imperial is, as usual, having plenty of trouble getting enough help—none of the girls seem to stay long. And no wonder—too damned much work.

Like Seattle, as the war flooded Everett with servicemen and war industry workers, even hotels as desperate as the Strand could feed on the crumbs of leftover prosperity. They stumbled over the threshold in faded dresses or Army Air Corps uniforms, stopping at the front desk as if asking permission to continue into the murky upstairs, where spirits clung to rooms humming with lost voices.

Sometimes they paused long enough to regale the bemused night clerk with a chorus of drunken singing; others passed a moment of friendly banter before treading noisily up the uncarpeted wooden stairs. Often, when he prepared a room for the next customer, Fox found an empty bottle on the nightstand, left behind like some used-up companion.

Even lying alone on her Seattle hotel bed, drawing hard on a cigarette and stubbing the butt into an ashtray beside her, Gracie must've recognized the voices of those travelers. They could just as easily be her own.

Often, when she read his letters, a $10 bill tumbled out the folds and she clutched it anxiously to her breast. Sometimes what tumbled out was much stronger currency, as he once wrote:

I came damn near phoning you the other night. It was like this: There were four or five people in the lobby, around 2 a.m. talking, laughing and passing the bottle. Then suddenly they all left, going either up to their rooms or out somewhere, and I found myself quite alone. I picked up a book, settled down comfortably in my favorite chair and began to read. I felt warm and nice from the several drinks I had inside me, and the world for the moment seemed a very pleasant sort of place. I read a page or two, when I noticed how awfully quiet it was—not a sound breaking the stillness. Then suddenly the strangest thoughts stirred up my mind for a moment, and leaving me with a sort of hazy impression that you were sick or in some kind of trouble. "I must call her up right now," I said to myself.

I actually got up and started toward the phone booth. And all at once that troubled feeling left me, left me standing in the middle of the lobby thinking what a foolish thing it would be to call you, when you were doubtless busy at work, out with some friends or otherwise snoozing comfortably in bed. To you I suppose all this seems rather silly—perhaps you'll think I was drunk. But it wasn't that.

One quite imagines Gracie sitting by a lampshade at a wooden desk near her hotel room window, listening to the steady heartbeat of his letters. Perhaps she lay on her bed. The window in the room must have looked out onto a sky hanging so low in winter it seemed to scrape bricks from the faces of Seattle's tallest buildings. Gathering up a fountain pen and using stationery designed with a "Full Speed Ahead to Victory" logo at the top, she summoned her thoughts.

Her words, as straightforward as a punch in the face, would never touch the eloquence of his, but then, that was just Gracie's style.

Dear Ed, How in the hell are you old top? By your letters there is never a dull moment at the Strand Hotel. But it would not seem rite if things were too quiet, it would not be a hotel if so.—Gracie

Hello Ed, I have been having a lot of trouble with my legs. They sure get worse when I'm on my feet. Sure is god damn disgusting. I don't mean maybe... Well, tell mother hello for me. Thanks for the money, sure comes in handy. I am having one hell of a time of it. As Ever,—Grace

Hello Ed, How are you today. I don't feel very good. I am staying in bed today.—Gracie

Dear Ed, Thank you honey for the lovely pearls, they are sure very nice.—Gracie

Hello Ed, How are you today? OK I hope, also your mother. Me, I did my hair up in curlers as I always do. I did the back a little short and had to make it tighter. Next morning when I took them out around the back of my neck was a bunch of little bumps. I did not pay any attention and went to work. When I came home had terrible headache. When I got up the following day I couldn't comb my hair they were as large as quarters turned into metal poisoning. I am having one hell of a time. I don't seem to heal.—Gracie

Hello Ed, Guess you began to think I had died. Not yet but dam near... I have had blood poison in my toe which was caused from a blister. Not very dam pleasant to have... Thanks for the books and smokes they are dam hard to get here. Here's kiss for you. XX.—Gracie

Dear Gracie:

    Have had a bit of old hell at the hotel lately. It all started a week ago last Saturday. When I got down there Saturday night, the 4 to 12 dame immediately started in with her tale of woe.

    The couple in No. 1 were raising hell—he was drunk and she was afraid to go up and say as much as one mild "boo" to him.

"I'll wait a bit and see what develops," I said, and started to count the money. Just then came a heavy bump from overhead, like a body falling off the bed. I continued to count money. Soon came a crash. The dame looked at me expectantly. I kept on counting until finished. Then came a loud cry and a crash again.

"I'm going up," I told her, "you hold the desk till I come down."

I went up…door not quite locked—a bit of a push and I was in the room, to the tune of a loud cry and heavy bump.

A red-haired guy in pants and undershirt had a gal on her back on the floor by the bed. His knee was planted into her belly and he was banging her head against the baseboard. Her black dress was twisted around, revealing a short stretch of pink garter, and one shoe was kicked off. He evidently didn't realize I was in the room until I had him by the hair and gave his head a sharp backward jerk. He swung about, a startled look on his face.

"What do you want?" he demanded.

He was pretty drunk. I told him to get up. He did; wanted to fight. I said not to make any more of a damned fool of himself than he had done already.

"You're going out, fella—make too much noise for the folks around here. Put on your clothes and disappear fast."

He whined; he would be quiet—he wouldn't disturb anyone. His wife (or whatever she was—the devil knows) started to cry—"I told you that you shouldn't drink any more. But no—you knew how much you could take. Yeah—and now see where you're at!"

This noise annoyed him—"For Christ sake shut up!" he shouted at her.

Finally he got on his jacket, and out and down they started. I helped him down the first few steps, but he seemed pretty steady on his pins so I let him go under his own power. All went well until he got to the bottom turn in the stairs. Instead of making the turn he did a head-on crash into the phone booth—right thru the glass. Glass flew all over the damned guy. "Now see what you've gone and done," shouted his dame.

Slowly he hauled himself out of the booth. He was frightened, and his hands shook as he tried to pick bits of glass off his jacket.

"I'm all cut up—I'm bleeding on my shoulder," he wailed. I jerked open his shirt. There was no blood anywhere; indeed he had escaped without one scratch— drunkard's luck by god. All this happened in about ten minutes, but I spent the

next half hour and more cleaning up broken glass. For that trouble I soaked him five bucks, which scarcely nicked the fat wad he was packing around.

The next night there was a gal sitting around the lobby when I got there, and she was putting on an act about being scared to death of sailors, her main occupation apparently being to keep distance between them and herself.

Finally she went out to eat, leaving her baby up in their room howling his little head off. Within the hour she was back, up and out again. I missed her coming in, being upstairs showing a party to their room. Much later, on my way back to the lavatory and which took me past her room, I thought I heard odd noises coming from inside, such as when a gal and a guy are playing a game which you won't find in Hoyle's book of card games either! The baby was howling again, too.

The boss is particular as hell about a guy being in a room with a dame unless registered Mr. & Mrs., but I thought it best not to disturb them until they'd finished their piece anyway. Then I knocked, and I'll be god-damned if out doesn't pop a sailor! What in the hell did I want? I told him to just keep walking. And he did. The dame begged me not to report her. She sat on the edge of the bed with a bit of sheet wrapped around her hips. I looked at the little baby bundled up in the bed, crying. It was sick, she told me.

"I guess you think I'm an awful person," she said presently. "But god!—I'm young, my husband's been in the navy almost a year—and my god, mister, if I don't get something once in a while I'll go nuts, that's all."

Well, dear Gracie Gal, enough of this for now. I hope this finds you much better. 'Bye now.—Ed

Gracie Gal reached for the wristwatch but her fingers came back empty. She sat up on the lumpy mattress and looked over to the nightstand. Her head pounded. The cute little Parker's Lady wristwatch with block numerals was gone. Damn. And more damn. Her head ached, her stomach fought rough seas, even her legs hurt. Her "graceful little legs," wasn't that what Ed Fox once called them? Now they were sore and tired and no use to anyone.

And she no longer had the watch. The watch *he* had given her. Damn.

Perhaps then she noticed the depressing stained walls of her Seattle hotel room. Perhaps she was just too hungover to care.

11

No stopping their laughter
(Japan, 1945)

THE DAYS PASSED with a familiar one-two jab, like a boxer working them over—three years, 36 months, 1,095 days, 26,280 hours, and counting. Always counting, always ducking those jabs.

By spring of that final year when Allied armies checked Hitler in Europe, all attention turned to the campaign in the Pacific. Still, the world seemed unprepared for the war's shocking end. The atomic blasts at Hiroshima and Nagasaki startled to the core of human understanding, but it was the B29 firebombs that most of the Japanese people would never forget. The climax, those who were there will tell you, burned itself in blood.

Nearly every night and into daylight as well, American B29s flew mostly unchallenged toward Japan's industrial cities, their bomb bays stuffed with fire.

Sometimes, with the huge, silver B29s nearly blotting out the sun, prisoners gleefully pointed skyward and shouted over the roar: "Ichiban." Number one. They were the biggest, loudest, most damning airplanes anyone had ever seen.

About a mile from the entrance to a Hitachi copper mine and its narrow, stony mountain trail, Galen Martin and the others spent their final months in wooden barracks that resembled Depression-era shacks. In the winter of this last year, he lay on his freezing bunk, and through cracks in the walls watched winds swirl eddies of dirt in the compound yard. The room's only warmth drifted out of a puny floor heater that was overmatched by the cold.

Somehow the prisoners scrounged together a crude crystal radio and at night they gathered in the darkness, secretly listening to the chatter of the B29 pilots overhead. The American voices, disconnected and staticky, comforted nonetheless. Sometimes there was mention of an island and the eager prisoners calculated the Allied advance. The firebombing was just the prelude. Soon, they believed, American ground troops would invade Japanese soil. Just wait, they whispered.

Other nights, with the growl of B29s low and terrifying, the anxious guards rooted them from their beds and into a tunnel drilled in a nearby hillside. "Sekitateru." Hurry, Hurry. Half-asleep and scared, the clumsy prisoners found the dark, clammy tunnel particularly unsettling, for they suspected that when the American invasion began, they might easily be pushed through that damp earthen opening, only to find the exit blocked by machine guns— one mass murder, one mass grave. So spread the rumor, and middle-of-the-night rumors had a way of turning up fact. It was as if you could hear a machine gun barking in that blocked-off tunnel and feel its bullets ripping sockets of flesh. It wouldn't be clean, Galen knew as much. No, it'd be wild, scattered shots sparking randomly off hard rock walls, eventually killing every last one of them.

Galen couldn't help but consider such possibilities as he sweated each day deep within the copper mine, a dark, suffocating place 15 levels beneath the surface of everything he knew.

The thin glow from his carbide miner's helmet cut weakly through the dim. His jackhammer drilled into the earth's core, spitting out chunks of debris and powder that coated his arms and pants. The air smelled of dust. Pounding from the heavy jackhammer rose up his arms and shoulders, shaking and shaking, until one day it seemed to loosen a connection in his brain and it all ran together—the night invasion of Corregidor, Cabanatuan, the rice fields of Japan.

"I'm tired," he shouted above the jackhammer's drumming, his miner's helmet flashing on the prisoner beside him. "Tired of this." So he sat and waited.

The mineshaft suddenly grew quiet. The two exhausted prisoners were quiet too, as if anticipating something—a shape, a sign, anything to change the direction of what was about to happen. Soon they heard the footsteps of two Japanese honchos. The honchos were civilian guards who carried just enough authority to make them mean. They snuck about the tight, low mine day after day, terrorizing those prisoners they caught resting and those simply working too slow in service to the Emperor's great war.

The footsteps approached. What happened next seemed to grow on its own and the two prisoners hadn't the power to stop it even if they'd wanted to.

Galen's fingers tightened around a dirty iron bar and he rose to his feet with surprising resolve. He snapped off his carbide light. He was ready now, controlled and dangerous, a shadow lurking far from judgement above. The footsteps crunched closer. Revenge was thick in the choking underground air. It was war and they were the enemy. In war you eliminate and forget. He waited for the footsteps, closer and closer. Light from the approaching helmets cast down on the hard mine shaft floor. He stepped from the shadows. When he swung it was with the force of three years and thousands of deaths, torpedoed hell ships, and overflowing burial fields. He swung because there was nothing else left in him to give—no more waiting, no more humiliation, no more watching your friends die badly. Maybe you just had to live through it to understand, and even then, when you turned it over later on, it lost some sense. The metal bar in his hands cracked hard into skullbone.

Then it was the other prisoner's turn and the job was complete.

Their miner's lights clicked back on. Outlined in the harsh artificial light lay two bodies.

Moving swiftly, the prisoners dragged one body, then the other, over the rocks to an ore shaft opening.

Close their eyes, make them sleep; quickly, quickly, down that deep black hole.

The honchos were weighty, unlike the skeletons in the death fields of Bataan, and they fell into the shaft as if they were heavy rocks tumbling down a well. The two prisoners filled a mine car with copper ore, pushed it into the opening and heard it crush bottom far below. They filled another car and another and one more still. There would be no toes wiggling, no arms or legs floating to the top of this grave.

It was war after all; they were the enemy. In war, you eliminate and forget.

Galen giggled. It was over. Soon their laughter echoed off the cave walls, their carbide lights shining a wild prehistoric dance. Two crazy men in a dark, dark place.

Now there was no stopping their laughter.

We kept telling them we're gonna' outlive you, you won't get the best of us.—Galen Martin

Jack lay in the cold gravel ditch, the familiar smell of seaweed drifting in from darkened Tokyo Bay. An enormous wave of distant yellow flame lit his face.

Never had he been witness to such a fire. Outside of hell none other existed. It was awful. It was beautiful. God, how it seared your heart.

Hour after hour, the B29s came in low and mean over Tokyo, their four engines growling vengeance. They were huge silver war machines, fast and nimble, able to deliver 10 tons of kill. Enemies would suffer before their fury.

America had discovered Japan's great weakness. Fire was its scourge. Homes constructed of paper, bamboo, and wood were built not even shoulder length apart and burned like kerosene, one igniting the next. Tokyo's neighborhoods, rising from the Sumida River as far as the eye could see, were separated only by fingers of canals and narrow roads with low-slung power lines.

The Japanese were war weary. They were exhausted from rations that cut their food supplies, until they scrounged like beggars or paid dearly at black market stalls. There existed no oil for heat or gasoline for cars. More and more of their lifeblood drained away to the unwinnable war. Already a generation of young men was lost. And then, worst of all, came the B29s—at night too, when it was blood on black, and fire over darkness.

Air raid alarms wailed. Tiny speakers fastened to power poles everywhere in Tokyo screamed empty warnings.

The first planes skimmed in that night of March 9, 1945, dropping bombs filled with napalm, a devilish mixture of jellied gasoline that clung to houses, carts, and clothes, and then burst into flame. The bombs exploded a hundred feet above the city, shooting out thousands of napalm cylinders. Soon a giant flaming X, visible for miles in the sky, burned Tokyo's Koto District. Next came the main body of planes, one every minute. From their bomb bays fell 500 pound clusters that exploded above, raining forth neon droplets of oil. Flames leapt up to greet the oil overhead and soon the hungry beast was in the air, spreading on the wind until rivers of fire gushed down streets.

The fire created its own 40 mph gusts that pushed through paper homes, their white wood skeletons silhouetted for a moment against the bright night before crumbling into incinerator ashes. The flames moved on. It was the sound of a hurricane. It was the roar of an animal. Panicked families ran towards the Sumida River, the hot suffocating fire breathing at their backs. To the river, to the river, they ran. Now flames lit the sky like a noontime sun, sucking oxygen from the air. To the river, to the river. Mothers with babies strapped on back couldn't know that their children were already dead. Weeping husbands searched among charred corpses. The Sumida canals boiled flesh—families steamed to death in the river's baptismal font. The fire moved on, refusing to stop and contemplate its work. It jumped across roads, it bullied past fire breaks, and on and on, creating weird updrafts that buckled the bomber formations that flew uninterrupted overhead. Soot blackened the underbellies of the late-arriving B29s and the smell of human flesh drifted into the cockpits.

The burnt streets leading to the river reeked of destruction. Temperatures reached 1,800 degrees. Charred bodies littered the way: a man and woman entwined in a final charcoal pitch embrace; a child's school cap in a pile of embers; a canal swollen with bloated remains.

The Japanese counted nearly 84,000 dead from that one night alone, more than 40,000 injured, and more than 250,000 buildings destroyed in Koto, Fukagawa, Mukojima, and Honjo districts. In one night alone—from such horror the Japanese were defenseless.

The Americans were thrilled. Leaflets warned of future firebombing raids. Soon it was Osaka, then Nagoya, eventually they would bomb the neighborhoods of Koriyama, Sendai, Shizuoka, Koizumi, Tachikawa, and Yokohama. Remember Pearl Harbor, never forget Bataan. On they came, forever it seemed, their bomb bays filled with hate.

Jack had a front row view as the bombers flew over his sorry prison camp on Yokohama's industrial waterfront, at times their fiery payloads lapping dangerously close to his warehouse barracks.

One spring night in 1945, as the air raid sirens blew, Jack ran from his sleeping bay and flopped into the ditch alongside other prisoners by the railroad tracks. For more than three hours the B29s came, converging on the industrial waterfront between Yokohama and Tokyo. They flew as low as

5,000 feet, where Jack could almost see the pilot's grim faces shining through the searchlights in the harbor and the flames of the burning buildings. Above the bombers, the white clouds were like the ceiling on a vast burning house, trapping the heat and pushing the smoke and flames back into the city below.

The incendiaries floated down, and licks of flame, racing from building to building, swallowed everything in their way. Children, their clothes aflame, ran screaming down hot Yokohama streets.

Speakers wired to power poles provided an eerie commentary.

"Bi Niju Ku." B29. "Bi Niju Ku. Bi Niju Ku. Bi Niju Ku." There were more than anyone could count. "Tak san Bi Niju Ku."

Through the deafening roar, Jack heard the distant clang, clang of little three-wheeled Japanese fire trucks. Each carried a tank of fire retardant, a driver, and a couple men hanging off the back. Throughout Yokohama the impotent clang was a joke against the great man-made inferno.

A searchlight traced the flight of a B29 across the smoky sky. Soon other searchlights locked the bomber in their crossbeams and Japanese Zeros, their running lights shining, flashed down from above. Tracer bullets spun red spider webs across the ruined city. An explosion followed and the B29's wing ripped off. And yet even in their last seconds, the doomed B29 gunners continued shooting, their tracers arcing angry orange rivets as the giant bird plummeted to its death into the flaming city below. It was quiet for a second, and then black smoke rose through the searchlight's triumphant beam.

Later, as the awesome fires raged and his senses could take no more, Jack left the gravel ditch and walked into the prison camp bathroom. The benjo was situated so you could stand before the toilet holes in the wood floor and peer through slits in the wall directly at Tokyo and Yokohama.

The bright flames outside formed shadows that crackled off the benjo walls. Jack stood silently for a moment, listening to the roar of the bombers and watching the cities burn beneath them. He glanced at a prisoner beside him. On the man's face, illuminated by the great distant conflagration, was a look of complete satisfaction.

In daylight, seeing the work of the firebombs was frightening and chilling. Blocks of rubble smoldered in the white ash of morning. A shrill breeze from the city blew about the odor of charred buildings. The Japanese had no an-swers for fire. They were running short on answers for war.

Jack took a deep breath, his lungs filling with the scorched air. The pris-oners were told they were moving. After nearly three years in the Yokohama camp, it was good to be leaving, even for another destination unknown and future uncertain.

They split up one day soon thereafter and marched past the familiar shops and bathhouse onto waiting trains, where the steady click of train wheels scoured his mind and he was free of the Yokohama waterfront. Again he found himself wedged alongside other prisoners, their unclean smell fill-ing every space of the car. Hanson with his long legs and lean, friendly face was there, as was Johannsen, making the circle complete. Everywhere prison-ers, everywhere anxiety and never ending hunger, and even the first threads of something that could almost be called hope. But even that brought about more worries. If the Americans did invade, what would the Japanese do with their war prisoners? What sort of retribution would they extract for those fire-bombs from the sky?

Click click, click click, the train's rhythm steadied his thoughts. He long ago had given up trying to understand.

Hours later the train rumbled to a stop before a sawmill in the mountains some 250 miles from Yokohama. Disappointment was what Jack had come to expect from Japanese slave labor camps, and this proved no exception.

Groups of prisoners, barely looking up at the new arrivals, shouldered in logs that others pushed through mill saws. Stacks of finished 4x4s piled up outside for use in air raid shelters elsewhere.

The men in their shabby prison uniforms were worn-out machines, mechanically finishing one load of wood and gathering in another.

Before long Jack was one of them, pulling pieces of wood through a 30 inch buzz blade. Sawdust sprayed his clothes and face and it hung like a win-try breath in the noisy building. Nearby through the great clatter, slack-faced prisoners hauled out fresh-cut boards.

Jack's attention focused on the spinning sawblade. He was close to the open disc and could feel it move, aware of its insatiable appetite. He knew to be wary. His hands reached out to spread another strip through it.

It'd been like that since he'd arrived. Breakfast of rice, then work, lunch of rice, and then more wood through the whirring blade, his blue eyes darting across the sawfield to more wood, more blade.

Only one time, and he learned it only takes one time, Jack's eyes betrayed him. Maybe it was the years of rice and water soup that weakened him so that the sawblade seemed further away, less threatening, less ready to claw out for him. His right hand, his high school quarterback's steady hand, ventured too close to the blade. With a shock he felt a viscous snap, a sudden angry bite. The shock convulsed in waves before his eyes. Blood from a severed finger splattered the wood. Streaks of blood. *My blood,* Jack thought, still not quite believing the fountain of red spurting from his right middle finger. An explosion of pain. Sawblades stopped. Wood chips hung suspended in air. Prisoners stared. A clumsy guard wrapped coarse string around his finger and Jack stumbled forward in a daze. Another guard pushed him toward camp, more than a mile away. He passed in and out. It wasn't real. It wasn't happening. Not to me, not now with those B29s so close to ending it.

The stringy tourniquet proved useless, so he clamped the finger with his other hand, squeezing tight to slow the blood's flow. "Sekitateru, sekitateru," the guard implored. But running only made the blood pump faster out his finger's bloody spigot. Even the air currents turned against him, forcing their way into his open wound. His hands dripped. He felt himself slipping away. How could this happen?

Back at the barracks waited a Dutch prisoner from Sumatra named Pyma, who possessed enough rudimentary knowledge to be considered the prison camp doctor. He summarily examined Jack's finger, severed at the first joint, and motioned him to the edge of a coarse wood table. The Dutchman ordered up a pot of boiling water to sterilize his primitive tools. It took forever, it seemed to Jack, who still disbelieved. There was no anesthetic, not even a swallow of sake to cut the pain.

Pyma's knife soon slashed deep gashes down each side of Jack's mutilated finger. Before long he'd filleted open the red flesh and pulled it back, exposing the ragged white bone, until the top third of his finger was just a joint of meatless bone. Pyma instructed another prisoner to clamp needle-nosed pliers onto the shattered fingertip.

Jack's breaths escaped in shallow grunts, sweat beading his worried face. The prisoner beside him squeezed raw bone in the pliers' grip. *Hurry, hurry,* Jack thought. *Oh God, hurry.* There wasn't even an aspirin tablet to cut the pain. The Dutchman's breath whistled through his nostrils. He calmly knifed through the rubbery bone as if he were trimming fat from a steak. Jack stared. The pliers bit.

An eternity later Pyma reached into the hot water and pulled out a crooked needle. He flopped the skin back over the trimmed endbone as if re-wrapping a package. Then he sewed, white thread through pink flesh. Up one side and down the other, pulling tight until the blood clotted at the end into a purple, angry bulb.

For the next couple nights, Jack rigged up a sling of rope and cloth to hold up his arm. It was the only way he found to stop the throbbing that pulsed through his hand all the way to the shoulder. There still wasn't so much as an aspirin to cut the pain.

A few days later a corpuscle of white popped through the end of the purple stump. Even the brush of loose cloth sent shooting pains through his hand. Jack decided it was a nerve exposed to the air and his only chance for relief was to cut it out. He braced himself. But Pyma discovered it was only a sliver of bone rubbing nerve. When he clipped it out, Jack felt a surge of relief.

Galen Martin wasn't surprised when the rocky grave was discovered under the carloads of heavy ore. For weeks he watched as the Japanese guards methodically searched the mine's maze of dark tunnels for the two missing honchos. It was only a matter of time.

The prisoners played dumb while the search continued around them. "What honchos?" their attitude suggested. Still, Galen knew he'd eventually be found out. The only surprise was that the Japanese officers didn't kill him on the spot. As it was, the execution orders seemed odd following years of un-checked violence toward the prisoners, starting with Bataan. They never bothered before with formal execution orders; they just pulled the trigger or swung the sword. Perhaps it was the threat of those B29s overhead that warned the prison camp officers that their Greater East Asia Co-Prosperity

Sphere was collapsing and accountability would rule some day in a foreign court. Even war has rules. At least it's supposed to.

It took search parties three weeks to find the honchos' bodies. Three weeks of nervous anticipation with an inevitable outcome that held Galen spellbound. He trudged to the mine every morning expecting that to be the day the bodies would be located under those four carloads of ore. Maybe the smell would lead their noses to the grave. He remembered how it felt dropping the warm, lifeless bodies down the black shaft. It was nothing like those skinny, childlike corpses he dumped day after day into the burial pits at Cabanatuan. At least now everyone knew the score. Maybe the score was evened a little.

When the excited shout of discovery arose from the lonely shaft, Galen squared himself for what lay ahead. Every evening for a week straight, he and the other prisoner from the mineshaft were tied to a big wooden post in the prison yard with their hands before them. They were bloody and bruised from the unrelenting beatings. At midnight they were cut loose and kicked back to the barracks. As he lay on his forlorn bunk and stared through cracks in the wall, he could see the wood post out there waiting.

Every day it seemed someone from camp reminded him of the execution orders. "How many days you got left?"

The execution orders told the story. On September 15, 1945, six weeks away, Galen would die.

The old train rattled on. Like the others sitting shoulder-to-shoulder in their filthy prison uniforms, Henry Chamberlain obediently ducked his head. But that didn't deter his eyes from the train's windows. Though the curtains were closed, the train's movements occasionally shook them open a couple inches and he caught glimpses outside. It was as if he were peeping through the slats in a fence.

Henry had listened to the nightly B29 firebomb raids over the great Japanese cities and imagined what sort of destruction he'd find should he pull back the curtains on the wobbly old train.

They were told to keep their heads bowed; to disobey invited the wrath of an impatient guard.

But as the train clattered on through the Tokyo metropolis, his downcast eyes snatched glimpses outside. The destruction was shocking. At that moment he wanted nothing more than to pull back the curtains and stare uninterrupted at the gray, flattened neighborhoods and the ruined waterfront factories. Enormous piles of rubble were strewn about the streets. With a start, he realized that what he was staring at out the train's window was complete and unconditional defeat.

Suddenly, as the train continued on, a flight of enormous B29 Superfortresses broke through the clouds on a daylight bombing raid. They were huge birds, so big they took your breath away. Beyond the curtains, Chamberlain saw sticks of bombs free-falling from the airplane bellies onto the defenseless city. The only resistance was the air between the planes and the houses. The end was close at hand, he was certain of it. The train rattled on.

They tried to keep it from us but we could see buildings down, streets torn up, rubble. That did more for our morale than anything, we knew they were getting their turn now.—Henry Chamberlain

Fran Agnes was working in a millyard when the air raid sirens broke. Their high-pitched screams meant little to him; he was accustomed to the sound. On this hot, sticky, August afternoon, however, he neither saw nor heard American planes. Still, the guards hurried the prisoners to a revetment area behind a pile of coal where they crouched until the all-clear signal blew.

Just another American air raid over Japan, he considered at first. Only then his eyes caught sight of the roiling black cloud mushrooming into the sky over Hiroshima, 35 miles away. It was like nothing he'd seen before.

"They hit an oil refinery," one of the prisoners muttered.

"Burning all right," someone else remarked.

Afterwards, the guards were unusually quiet. Before long a Japanese officer rode up on a bicycle. The guards exchanged words. Soon the prisoners marched back to camp. In the middle of the afternoon; that was strange. Fran retraced his steps down the dusty road. Very strange. A breeze from Hiroshima blew his way, but all he smelled was hot afternoon air.

Back at camp the prisoners cleaned up and ate their rations. Oddly, the guards seemed distracted, weren't nagging as usual.

The camp's interpreter, a Japanese man in his late 40s who was too old to fight and had lived most of his life in California, signaled a prisoner to meet him behind the barracks.

"Killed 100,000," his finger traced into the dirt.

"We don't have a bomb that could do that," the prisoner replied.

The interpreter pointed again to his markings in the dirt. Then he erased it with his shoe.

Galen heard strange talk on the crystal radio as the prisoners huddled around in the darkness. Occasionally the pilots made vague references to a super bomb. The camp interpreter told them of a killer that exploded like a lightning sun onto Hiroshima, unleashing a strange hot cloud that rose toward the heavens. The heat of the awful new weapon vaporized thousands, he said.

A few days later, Galen learned of the second atomic blast, this one at Nagasaki. He had no idea what it was, but from the look on the guard's faces it was bad. Bad for the Japanese meant good for the prisoners.

"Hey, Martin, how many days you got left?"

They damn well better hurry, he thought.

12

Unconditional surrender
(Everett, 1945)

 Job Completed, A Jap Defeated.—sign posted on a Paine Field hangar

Well kid, the war's not over yet, but the big day is definitely getting closer. With the atomic bomb coming down on their heads and the Americans closing in on the one side and the Russians on the other, it doesn't seem possible that the little sons' o' Heaven can hold out very much longer. Most of the boys in the service with whom I've talked seem happier than in many months. And who in the hell can wonder at that—they've sure had a hell of a time of it, even those coming back and not wounded. As for those poor devils all torn apart yet still living, well, no words can adequately describe how they feel.—Ed Fox, August 10, 1945

On August 15 at 4 p.m. Pacific War Time, President Harry Truman announced to the world that Japan had surrendered. Unconditionally.

In downtown San Francisco, parading servicemen and civilians built huge bonfires on city streets. They sacked a liquor store and commandeered trolley cars.

In Denver, a celebrating soldier fell out a third story hotel window and died.

At 2 a.m. in St. Louis, crowds of people beat pans, blew whistles, and persuaded a parish priest to open his church for mass.

Everett had never seen anything like it, or scarcely would anytime soon. The automobile horns were so loud you could barely hear the waterfront mill whistles, surely the first time that the ubiquitous whistles, the city's symbol of order and establishment, were ignored.

"Have you heard? The Japanese surrendered. Unconditional."

After four years, the homefront had shifted—settling to the amazing war overseas and the ways it had shaped everything.

While the number of criminal cases in the Everett area had been cut in half, divorces continued at nearly double the wartime rate. Following whirlwind courtships, or so explained a common theory, homesick soldiers had simply married too fast. Others believed that the sudden prosperity from defense plant wages had somehow spawned domestic unhappiness.

World War II was a time when book circulation numbers at the Everett Public Library declined steadily and women were told: "Beauty Is Your Duty, Look Pretty Please." It was a time when housewives conscientiously saved their cooking grease, which was collected and used to make gunpowder. "Until the Japs are licked, we must keep on saving used fats," the government insisted.

On the radio there was Abbott and Costello, Bing Crosby, Jack Armstrong, Red Ryder, and The Lone Ranger. Somewhere inside a typical two-story house, which sold for about $5,000 in Everett, you might find Fletcher's Castoria, cod liver oil, Stag After Shave, and Doan's Kidney Pills.

For a while at the beginning, the war was so pervasive that even Everett's weather was a military secret, and for more than a year the local newspaper was ordered to drop its daily forecast lest it fall into enemy hands for planning an attack.

To relieve congestion on rail lines for war goods, Budweiser beer was no longer being shipped to the West Coast. "In the busy meantime, we commend to our friends the many fine beers now being brewed on the Pacific Coast," the beer maker told its customers. At the time, Sicks' Select and Rainier were brewed in Seattle. Also available was a concoction known as "Victory Beer."

The nationwide war bond drives scheduled at least once a year were trumpeted by full-page newspaper ads. The ads were mean, vengeful, emotional, and altogether successful.

There were grotesquely drawn Japanese soldiers with huge buck teeth and thick glasses: "Make him remember. We need more guns, planes, tanks. Buy extra bonds this week."

There was a beautiful, smiling, curly-haired girl with a birthday cake in the background: "I'm coming to your house to tell you about my daddy in a Jap prison. I've never seen my daddy. For more than a year he's been a prisoner of the Japs. I want him back for my next birthday. Will you help me? I don't want to grow up without my daddy. Buy War bonds."

"Come on Everett," still another exclaimed. "Send a dollar to bomb Tokio! $1 in war stamps from every American will build the mystery ship Shangri-La. A tremendous new aircraft carrier that will soon point its nose toward Tokio—the idea is to have every American man, woman and child buy one dollar's worth of war stamps—and the money thus raised will buy the new 'Shangri-La!' The Shangri-La will be terrific! It will be huge. It will carry death and flames and vengeance into the very heart of Japan! Since Pearl Harbor, since Bataan, since the unspeakable murders of our captured fliers, every American has itched for a chance to take a crack at Japan. This is your personal chance. Your carrier, your baby, your Shangri-La will hurl that spare change of yours, that big important dollar smack in Tojo's face."

In the winter of 1944, the *Shangri-La*, a 27,000-ton, $66 million aircraft carrier, was launched in Norfolk, Virginia.

For some, homefront Everett was a time of trust, contentment, even silliness. There were children and circuses, Saturday matinees and running to the grassy banks of the Snohomish River for fishing and swimming. Front doors were unlocked. For a while, Everett police slapped notices on theater screens warning patrons that they faced a fine of $300 and 30 days in jail for spitting beans through straws at movie patrons. This after the glasses of a moviegoer had been shattered one weekend by a wild bean shot.

Sometimes there just was loss.

In May 1945, four months before the war's end, Second Lieutenant Margaret Billings, a graduate of Everett High and the Providence Hospital School of Nursing, became the first woman from Everett to die in the war. She was a nurse on the USS *Comfort*, a hospital ship attacked by a Kamikaze plane one night near Okinawa. Billings was at her post in surgery when the Kamikaze pilot, in defiance of all rules of war, circled a few times and then attacked the plainly marked hospital ship. As the Kamikaze circled overhead, searchlights played over the giant red crosses that were painted on the gleaming white decks and superstructure. Twenty-nine died that night, including six navy nurses. Back home, her parents read about the attack in the *Everett Daily Herald*. Hour after excruciating hour passed without official word. Finally, six days after the *Comfort* was attacked, the family received notification from the War Department. Another Everett resident dead, another gold star on the Everett High School flag.

And then, one day just three months from the war's end, an Everett family welcomed home a son from frontline duty in Europe. A few hours later on that very day, the War Department informed them their other son had died in combat in the Pacific.

On the afternoon of the Japanese surrender, stores and restaurants in downtown Everett closed their doors and thousands of cars spontaneously streamed along Hewitt and Colby avenues over pavement littered with streamers of paper that poured out of office windows.

Some of the cars drug strings of tin cans that clattered annoyingly behind them. The theaters on Colby were packed. Practically everything else was closed, so there was no place for the merry-makers to go but around and around, in defiance of four years of gas rationing. Several reckless drivers were booked into the police station.

Three days later, the 35 mph national speed limit was lifted. It had been in place since September 1942.

Meat would continue to be rationed for a while, as would sugar. Nylons though, those precious, lovely, smooth nylons, soon would be available downtown at Chaffee's.

At a little after 2 A.M., the noise suddenly ended, the taverns closed, and the town buttoned down.

Everyone went home and crawled into bed, happy and victorious. "The war is over, have you heard? Unconditional!"

13

Come home whistling

*T*HE HOUR OF LIBERATION began like all the other days for Henry Chamberlain, who saw freedom through barbed wire fences, but felt only the oppression of another day, another scratch on the calendar.

Who was to say, though, that this day would end like all the others?

At noon the camp commander stood on a box in the blazing heat. A line of raggedy prisoners waited behind him.

"Our Emperor say war over," he told them finally, his flat voice drifting without emotion, his words spreading disjointed across the prison yard until they came back together and made sense. "You go home."

That was it. Eight words. Eight glorious, unbelievable words. He stepped down from the wood box that had made him taller, turned, and stiff-walked back inside his small headquarters.

The sun still shone shadow to light. The air, unchanged from a moment earlier, held the same golden promise of late summer. The earth, the ugly prison camp earth, disclosed nothing. The tired Japanese flag with its rising sun drooped limply at its flagpole. A defeated flag, a sad, sorry flag if you really thought about it.

Henry lingered in the dusty compound yard, biting off pieces of understanding from the message just delivered.

He didn't know how to act; there'd been no preparation or training for this moment. And so, like any day, he awaited orders. It was all he knew. The sky hadn't parted, the earth didn't open, or Mount Fuji crumble before him.

It might've stayed suspended like that for quite some time, except one Marine, a tough buck sergeant whose father once served in an Asian embassy, decided to test the message.

"If you bastards don't have the guts to find out, I will," he snorted at a handful of American officers.

He tramped past a knot of Japanese guards. He didn't salute and they didn't stop him. Remarkable. Maybe it really was true, maybe the war was over. Soon he was at the commander's office, bounding up the three steps leading onto the porch.

Henry heard him growl before he'd reached the top step. His voice carried the haunting of cogon grass graveyards. It was the gravelly edge of payback. The Japanese commander emerged from his office and saluted. Saluted a prisoner?

Henry was thunderstruck. But that was nothing. As soon as the salute was lowered, the Marine delivered a roundhouse punch to his jaw. The Japanese commander picked himself up. The Marine felled him again.

The POWs watched in disbelief. The American returned to the compound, a huge grin spread across his sunny face.

Two Japanese guards jumped to attention.

Some of the 50 gallon barrels that dropped out of American airplanes were stuffed too tightly with food, cigarettes, letters, and medical supplies and thus overwhelmed their parachutes. The liberated prisoners playfully dodged the fat barrels that fell through the buzzing tailwind of those fading planes. When they splattered onto the rocky mountainside near Jack Elkins, cans of fruit cocktail split open.

Fruit cocktail was a miracle. Any western food, anything besides plain unsalted rice and fish head soup was a miracle. The prisoners gorged without shame. In one camp, a barrel packed with chocolate and canned milk exploded into one sugary mess that the men poured into cauldrons, heated, and drank. Their tongues had forgotten the sweet seduction of sugar.

It would take weeks to locate and remove the liberated prisoners sown throughout the ashen, firebombed country. Hidden in various nooks were more than 150 camps of Allied prisoners. Jack had a hard time thinking of himself as a former prisoner, a notion that hadn't sunk in completely and wouldn't for some time. In his mind he was still prison camp bones, a Marine who should've died in a Corregidor foxhole or inside those Yokohama barracks. It was only some kind of bizarre purpose that carried him through and spat him out at the other end.

He recalled Roy A. Wederbrook, who perished inside his machine gun nest overlooking the scarred Corregidor beachfront. His young, lifeless body lay atop several inches of spent brass machine gun casings.

"Ain't backin' up," Wederbrook's voice would occasionally ping pong through Jack's head, a reminder of how it all started. He promised himself to let Wederbrook's people hear that voice too, one last time, back in the Panhandle country of Texas. He wouldn't rest easy until that job was done, until that voice was put to sleep in his head.

He recalled Joe Gear from the Japanese hell ship, surely about to die, but defiantly exclaiming, "See ya' on Market Street." A few months before the end of the war, a letter arrived in the Yokohama barracks addressed to Hanson. He tore it open and read, a look of wonder spreading across his face. He gave it to Jack to read. It was from Joe Gear. That's right, Joe Gear, the very same corpse of a man who'd spent all those days tied to a ship's plank on the trip over, his poncho flying about in the open wind. They'd left Gear for dead on a Japanese dock. Unbelievable, Joe Gear was going home. Jack and Hanson stared at each other in amazement.

Jack dipped hungrily inside the broken containers. Sweet thick syrup dripped from his chin onto his chest. He ate too much too soon, but there were no limits now.

He sank his hand into another container of fruit.

The air was clear on this side of the mountain, where he and his mates from Yokohama had been ordered for the final weeks of the war. Birds chattered in distant trees. It could've been serene if he'd been in a mood to enjoy nature. Instead he was thinking of more immediate needs: food, rest, and then more food. The American cigarettes were delicious and he drew smoke deep into his lungs, pushing out the Japanese air.

In a couple days, Jack, Johannsen, and Hanson would take off on their own, scrounging through the Japanese countryside for food, waiting for the Americans to finally arrive. They had waited 42 months; they couldn't wait forever.

The Japanese civilians seemed afraid of them, and handed over what simple foods they could to the three skinny Americans. The liberation of pigs and chickens, Jack called it.

It wasn't the civilians he blamed or hated, it was the Japanese military.

Later, in the Navy hospital in Guam, he and Hanson could eat all they wanted, and whatever they wanted, any time, day or night. The fresh white bread washed down with glasses of whole milk was so rich it tasted like cake.

Jack had been gone so long, he couldn't let himself think of home. He was a little nervous about that whole situation anyway. Everywhere else the Allies had won. There'd be parades for the winners, but what would they do about Marines who surrendered? Would they sneak them back through Canada and so cover up their stain on the great Allied victory?

Home began to seem a damned complication. For now it was better to eat fruit cocktail and rest up for whatever else the world had in store.

The day Galen knew it was over, that it was finally and formally over, a POW swaggered into the camp commander's office, saluted, and punched him full in the face.

The American marched the commander past the cheering prisoners and into a shed. The door was shut behind him and then locked.

Look, see. Have you heard the Japs gave up? It was *they* who surrendered this time. The war is over. Hallelujah.

In the coming weeks, the Americans arrived in waves to liberate the prisoners, some 32,000 throughout all Japanese-held territories. The prisoners' condition was shocking, their stories even more unbelievable. Henry Chamberlain weighed about 80 pounds. Others could barely walk.

After the surrender, some prisoners held simple memorial services and waited for the Americans to arrive. Others overran their camps, broke into food storehouses, and tore into International Red Cross packages the Japanese had been hoarding for years. Packages that rightfully should have gone to the captives years earlier.

Some of the prisoners gorged, vomited, and ate more, their shrunken bodies rejecting the sudden overload of rich western food. Still, they couldn't stop. Later on, troop transports headed home or to hospitals in Guam and

Staff Sergeant Galen Martin, shortly after the war.

Hawaii, the mess decks were open around-the-clock for the ex-prisoners, who marveled at the piles of toast, jam, bacon, ham, steak, mashed potatoes, ice cream, candy, butter, stews, and soups.

In what seemed the cruelest twist of all, a couple planeloads of liberated prisoners, who had just survived years of captivity with the dream of home keeping them alive, died when their planes crashed during a sudden typhoon.

The ex-prisoners fanned out across America in hospital trains from Oakland, California. Inside were nurses in clean white uniforms, the cleanest vision yet of home. The friendly nurses absolutely radiated. And yet already the former prisoners were beginning to feel like outsiders. The harmonic voices marching out of hospital radios were uncomfortable and distracting, nothing like they'd remembered. There were songs never before heard and movies never seen. FDR had died and left honest Harry Truman in charge. Everything had changed. Everyone meant well, but America hadn't waited and they weren't sure why.

When one train laid over a few hours in Portland, Oregon, the ex-prisoners disappeared in small groups into the city streets. They smoked cigarettes and slammed liquor. There was something about the look on their faces that warned civilians away. They were chasing after a lot of missing time, searching for something to soften that hardness inside.

Several had to be snuck, stiff as boards, through the dark back onto the train.

One of those trains arrived late one night at Fort Lewis, near Tacoma, Washington, and the former prisoners of the Japanese climbed sleepily into trucks that took them inside a compound surrounded by a fence topped with barbed wire. The gate snapped shut behind them. In response to their disappointed looks, they learned they would be quarantined for a month in the same compound German war prisoners recently occupied.

"Bullshit," Odas Greer muttered. Prisoners again. Captives forever.

Greer ached for home. It was less than 70 miles up Puget Sound near Everett, where the gray clouds parted and a soft moistness blew in from the water. He hadn't been home in close to seven years. As he remembered, the land was emerald green with cedars, firs, ferns, and maples, their leaves streaked red, but not yet winter dead. The green overwhelmed him with memories so strong it nearly pulled him through the barbed wire north to where his mother lived.

After a few days quarantined at Fort Lewis, more than a dozen chipped in back pay one night and bribed a ward boy into leaving a door unlocked.

Greer stuffed his barracks bag with Army-issue clothes and essentials. He dressed in a snappy creased uniform and looked himself over. Ready at last.

Under the friendly darkness, the men slipped from the barracks and over to a fence surrounding the compound. They silently dug until there was room enough to slip under with their bags in tow. Soon Greer found himself on highway blacktop, his new army shoes holding sure to the hard surface. Round headlights momentarily lit his face.

He stuck out his thumb. The car stopped. Before long he could see Seattle in the distance, its horizon glowing a shiny neon optimism. On they drove, past Boeing Field, where the airplane company was destined to grow beyond imagination. Past the King Street and Union stations, where packed trains unloaded thousands of returning veterans who strode confidently into their new lives, the brightest future ever.

Nothing dared hold America back. Puget Sound cities seemed ready to tackle any challenge. Already Greer was a step or two behind, like everyone was running and he was stuck in mud.

The driver of the car had questions that Greer deflected in a polite way. It was friendly banter he wanted and Greer kept it at that. Smoke from his cigarette curled up, hiding his face. It was like pulling up a blanket. You ducked your head inside the warm cocoon and lost yourself. Japan was a place that would stay locked up inside like that, perhaps always.

The fellow offered to drive him to his mother's doorstep.

"No, stop here, I'll walk."

The car retreated into the night, its headlights finally snuffing out down the road. Greer slipped the barracks bag over his shoulder. His heart began racing.

He remembered the letters he'd received from his mother in prison camp and supposed she'd written hundreds more that never made it through the Japanese censors.

Everything is fine, everyone is OK. Love, mother. Oh, how he'd wanted to tell her he was OK too, that he would pull the prison blanket over his head and some day it'd all be over. *Everything is fine, everyone is OK. Love, mother.*

His shoes crunched gravel. Then he could see it: home, a shining lighthouse surrounded by dark sea. The old neighborhood was quiet. The strong peat aroma of the early Northwest autumn filled him.

Whenever he returned, no matter how long he'd been missing, Greer, an only child, signaled his mother by whistling, loud and clear, strong enough that she could hear even from inside.

Now he moistened his lips and began to whistle. Low at first, then louder, as his footsteps carried him away from prison camp and out of Japan. Just whistling, just joyous whistling to melt away the years of misfortune. Just whistling loud and clear.

A door burst open and for a second the back light illuminated the silhouette of a woman and then she was running to him, her lost child. Her only child.

Just whistling, mother, that's all it is. Just come home whistling.

They arrived, all three of them, at the Army hospital to show him home to dinner. Jack slipped into the backseat beside the daughter, proud of his sharp new Marine khakis, his skinny legs barely touching the perfect crease.

Before long their car deserted the trim hospital grounds and geared up through Oakland, the mother and father in the front seat tour guiding past the bay and the scrubby foothills of Northern California. The mother, who volunteered at the big military hospital, had invited Jack for Sunday dinner. He eagerly accepted and then wondered why.

Listening to them talk now, he felt the warm fall sunshine rainbow through the old automobile's windows. The engine hummed. The words drifted back and settled comfortably over him. They were a nice, back-home family. Everyone smiled and that seemed to sandpaper the awkward off him.

But when they entered the house, he was caged up. Forty months squatting with dirty mess kit tins in the company of camp flies and dying men does funny things to your head. Even when you pushed the thoughts down one side, they bubbled up somewhere else.

Open your yap and some hybrid Jap-English word might just slip out before you can swallow it back and think it over. Careful now, or you'll have to explain it all, even those parts best left unsaid.

While he sized up all the ways he didn't belong, the husband and wife politely masked their stares, good people that they were. Their daughter was done up bright, he noticed that too, a woman about his own age with a face he'd soon forget.

Maybe it was intended as a date, he supposed that's what it was, and his appraisal of her was more curious than anything. He hadn't thought about women in that way for a long time. It'd worried a lot of the other fellows who wondered, amongst everything else, if they'd ever again feel that basic animal drive. In prison camp, one appetite dulled all else and it was the overwhelming passion for a decent meal—fresh baked bread, ham with sweet mustard, pan-fried chicken with gravy and greens—dreams, all of it.

The jitters grew with each passing minute. He shouldn't have come. He fumbled with his silverware. He sipped wine. He picked at the food. He should be back at the hospital with the others.

He flitted from chair to chair. He lit a cigarette. He could feel their eyes on him, feel also the tension that rose through the room. He moved again. What was it that made the lady think he'd be a catch for her daughter? What made any mother think that? No one, not even Jack himself, had inventoried the damage in his head. In the hospital in Guam, a grinning newsman with a big box camera came along snapping pictures of the liberated prisoners, who more resembled foreign refugees than Marines. Afterwards someone showed Jack the picture and he couldn't believe the image glaring back at him—the cornered cat eyes, the gaunt face searching desperately for a place to hide.

And at the time he was just starting to feel wholeness return to his arms and legs. But it was counterfeit strength, weight without muscle, doughy flesh like that of an infant. He'd tried chinning himself over a bar and couldn't even lift his heels.

Looking around him, Jack understood how exiled he was from this world of soft chairs, reading lamps, and radios, and wondered if he'd ever gain passport back. Maybe

Jack Elkins in a Guam Army hospital, just weeks after liberation.

he'd seen too much, maybe he'd done more than any man could explain in polite company. Against his will, mocking his mightiest efforts, he felt himself disengaging and all those yesterdays rushed together into one broken-down misery in his head.

It was all time stolen, Jack firmly believed, when he totaled it up and the sum came crashing down on him that Sunday afternoon on the celebration of his 24th birthday.

We'd been gone so long in the back of your mind you sort of wondered if they hadn't broken your plate. We thought they'd written you off a long time ago. The closer I got to home the more anxious I got. I wasn't thinking about home, I'd been in there so damn long it seemed like I'd read where people had clean sheets and sat at a table, used knives and forks. We didn't have any chairs, just squatted on our haunches. We were so out of touch with anything that people considered normal.

I told you about the family in California who took me home for my birthday, the most uncomfortable three or four hours that anyone had ever spent. I was off the airplane, just back from the POW camp. I was like a caged animal, I hadn't been in a house, I hadn't sat in a chair, I didn't know how to use a knife and fork, and I could tell they were thinking "what are we gonna do with this guy?"

They were really good to me, had a nice dinner, took me around and showed me the sites of Oakland, but when it was over I'm sure they looked at each other and went "whoo, glad that's over."

It was the first time I'd been in a house since 1940.—Jack Elkins

There were more reunions than Galen Martin could remember and all the relatives wanted stories. After a while he'd just disappear, right in the middle of a party, just flat out leave like a man without footprints.

Fran Agnes felt pretty good about himself. He made it, and there was a lot to be said for that. He beat *them* in the end. At times he'd been so hungry he'd

even craved the taste of stale toothpaste sweetened up with a dab of sugar. But those days were over.

He'd held on and discovered that simple strength was all he had and the Japanese weren't going to wrench that away, too.

Keep moving, don't look back, don't stumble.

The rest of his life would be easy, just wait and see.

Back home on 90-day Army leave, he eventually called on the mother of an old high school friend. The last he'd seen of him, Fran was departing Cabanatuan by hell ship for Japan. He'd left the young soldier some salt and other meager items. Later, he learned his friend was prisoned in the hold of a rusty Japanese hell ship when an American submarine blew it out of the water.

And now Fran found himself in the house of his friend's mother, telling her as gently as possible what he knew to be truth.

"No," she shook her head. "My Glenn's gonna' come walking through that front door."

She stood her ground, proud and resolute, and guilt fell heavily on Fran's shoulders. His confidence dissolved. He read her thoughts clear as a Western Union telegram:

Why are you alive and others are not? Why did they die in prison camp and here you are feeling good about yourself? Why did some lose their arms and eyes and minds and you're still whole? What makes you so special?

Henry Chamberlain coiled into the cool dark cocktail lounge. It was early in the new year, 1946, and orange trees studded the wide breezy Los Angeles boulevards. It was a city without winters, an idea that grew into a metropolis of cars and jet airplanes and moving too fast. America wore a new attitude that started here, in a place famous for glittery illusions. After a few hours in an inky Los Angeles barroom, the glare off those tropical trees stung your eyes, so it was easier inside, like walking through life wearing sunglasses.

After a while, Henry found himself drifting along wherever a stream of scotch carried him. Liquor medicated his memories, drowning the screams that echoed through the *Haro Maru's* hold.

There is no future in a hell ship; tomorrow's empty, today everything and awful. Click the switch and shut it down.

He couldn't believe how America had changed. It was as if the earth shook sometime in the early 1940s and he never felt it. He told a surprised clerk he didn't want any *woman* measuring him for a new suit. A few weeks earlier, a woman sold him a car, the first since his return. It was all so strange. He tried swimming through the embryonic fluid that held four lost years of popular songs he'd never heard, jokes that disappeared, radio programs now just static in the atmosphere. Fibber Magee and Molly were over the war, why wasn't he? Jack Benny, Bing Crosby, and Frank Sinatra were over the war. It was old news; it was time to put it away in a drawer somewhere and have fun. Skitcheroo, kid. Let someone else worry for a change.

Henry found a low table inside the dark lounge, ordered his scotch, and awaited an old prewar friend. He sipped his drink while laughter slapped in waves across the room. Tobacco fumes burned his face.

He sometimes found himself going out at night only to awaken the next morning in a strange room. He couldn't remember where he'd been or why he'd been there. Maybe it was the scotch and maybe it wasn't so bad. There were other things he couldn't remember. The train ride from Bilibid Prison to Cabanatuan, for instance. When he was pushed standing up into the scorching boxcar alongside prisoners with shit dripping down their pant legs, his malaria-fevered mind had closed down, sparing him details. Like that switch again, just clicked off.

His friend spotted him from across the smoky room and approached through the gloom. Henry hadn't seen him. The background rustle of voices and glasses hid his footsteps and the man thought he'd surprise his old friend. In a moment he reached the table where Henry sat with his scotch. He clasped the back of Henry's shoulder warmly, two men who hadn't seen each other in a long time. A lot of water under the bridge.

Henry seized the hand. He felt a rush in his head. In a panic he leveraged his weight and flung his friend onto the bar table. Breathing hard, he stood over the prone body. He was back in Zero Ward. He was in the jungle of Bataan. He would never surrender again.

"My God," his friend exclaimed, looking up at him from the shambles of the table. "What a handshake."

Ever since, wherever he was, Henry made a point of sitting with his back against the wall. No one or no thing would ever sneak up from behind again.

It came over me like that, like a jolt. You drift back into civilization, but it didn't last very long. If you thought about it much, that is what would destroy you. You drive it out or you give up to it and let it destroy you.—Jack Elkins

14

Never buy green bananas
(summer 1991)

*I*T SHOULD'VE BEEN SO EASY, but somehow it got all tangled up.

Even half a century later, young Roy Wederbrook remained unfinished business, a nagging burr of regret. And so Jack returned sure as any pilgrim to the feed yards and sorghum bins that marked Wederbrook's hometown in the rolling Texas Panhandle. Only this time, he knew for certain, there'd never be another chance.

Jack had visited Hereford, Texas, before. It was the winter of 1951 when he'd come to finish with Wederbrook's family, perhaps even to eulogize the young Marine, a hero to Jack's way of thinking. But it unfolded badly that first time around.

He'd come down that February morning 40 years earlier riding a milky white 1950 Ford that cut a clean, ghostly blur through the stubbled fields along US 60. Hereford would've been just another farm town between the villages of Black and Dawn except Jack had purpose and the asphalt held true.

He'd been wintering in sunny Malibu that year when those Great Plains beckoned. What followed were long distance telephone calls, and then a half-baked marriage proposal to a young woman named Gladys. Now she simmered in Kansas City, considering the prospect of sharing her life with a man such as him.

After one of those late night calls, Jack packed his Ford and set out east over the cold winter prairie with his mind made up on two accounts: finish with Wederbrook, and hustle off to Kansas City to make that marriage offer stick.

For miles the white car purred through silo towns and winter fields so endless they seemed to freeze into the sky on the vast plain. He tried forming images into words. He fully intended to begin "He was a good Marine," and end somewhere with "Ain't backin' up no further." That last part, those words that said it all, could well be chipped into granite over R.A. Wederbrook's grave, wherever it was.

Wederbrook's mom lived on the outskirts of Hereford in a one-story farmhouse stubbornly ignoring the encroaching neighbors. During the war, a fenced camp of captured Italian soldiers rose out of the nearby grassland and its strong reminder clung yet to the broken fields. She must've thought of her son often, his memory as innocent as a child.

She was eager to meet Jack; he recognized it in her voice, friendly and plain spoken over the gas station telephone when he called for directions that morning. A chill blew across the treeless fields and tore through his coat when he hurried out the gas station door.

He decided Wederbrook's mom should know that, during lulls in the flashing artillery from Bataan, her son pick-axed a gun nest into the rock bluff overlooking the beach, and then hauled down belt after belt of .30 caliber bullets on a little trail he'd worn into the grassy bluff. Soon there wasn't much left in his world, just man, machine gun, bullets, and purpose. Good, happy-go-lucky Roy Wederbrook took a stand and Jack admired him for it. Right then and there, he promised, he'd tell as much if he survived and got the opportunity. At the time, with artillery crackling the air around him, neither seemed likely.

So it was that night, when the Japanese infantry attacked Corregidor's beaches, the serenade from Wederbrook's machine gun kept Jack centered as a compass needle that points north. But sometime in the insane firefight while the enemy bulled through a wall of bullets and clawed up the impossible rocky bluff, Wederbrook's gun grew silent.

A patrol of prisoners burying their dead a few days later found him crumpled atop those spent bullet casings, his shirt missing, his skin already beginning to pucker like overripe meat.

Wederbrook's mom ushered Jack into the kitchen, where the warm midmorning smells of baking and fresh coffee seemed to civilize the winter outside. The kitchen, he surmised, was the main room of the farmhouse and she its aproned matron. It recalled black woodstoves and long farm kitchen counters back home, where women's strong fingers shaped bowls of flour into smooth white dough. The big plain table where they sat was worn smooth from years of elbows and callused hands. That, and long-departed voices and soft yellow light from the kitchen window, mellowed it under a layer of polish. He imagined Wederbrook at this very table: histories told and lessons learned. It was a good place.

But before Jack settled much into his story, he realized with a start that Wederbrook's mom believed her son was alive. It was in her eyes and on her lips, the way she first took his hand with a stirring of friendliness and longing. It was in the way she shrank back as if bracing for a blow when he approached the telling of her son's final stand.

She'd been served official government notice—there was no hiding the truth, no mistaking the body in that machine gun stronghold. But an invisible energy held sway in that house and Jack decided he wouldn't soil her hope. No, he couldn't. Maybe she needed it, and maybe, like her son, she wasn't backing up either. No one could blame her for this.

Jack swallowed the strong bitter coffee and nibbled cookies that lost their taste. After a time measured long enough to be polite, he thanked her, said it was a pleasure knowing her son, wished her well, and left Hereford, Texas, to its cattle fields and feed lots, and another lost thread of his own life just now beginning again.

His white Ford sped towards Kansas City, failure stealing through the car's cracks, taunting his wounds. Jack's fingers gripped the steering wheel. He realized how desperately he'd wanted to say her son died bravely and with purpose. Not just Wederbrook, but all of them. She needed to understand how it was in a foxhole a million miles from nowhere, where dreams are not for miracles, just an honest messenger saying it hadn't been wasted. He wanted to shout it, to scream it out for everyone to hear.

Thus had Hereford, Texas, withered inside him 40 long years, until one spring Saturday in the early 1990s, when he found himself in Texas for an ex-POW convention. He boomeranged back to Hereford that day, unknown and unannounced, with Gladys alongside him this time, making sure promises made are promises kept.

They discovered the Veterans of Foreign Wars post several yards off the highway, partially hidden. The sign over the building stopped him. It read: R.A. Wederbrook VFW Post 4818. Imagine that. Maybe they already know the story, he thought. If so, it wasn't by his account.

When they entered the VFW club from the parking lot, Jack's eyes immediately found the portrait. Even from a distance of five decades he recognized the face. It was Wederbrook in his good greens. He looked like a million bucks up there over the fireplace mantle, young and handsome and sadly full of life. Jack came to pay respects to a man and was instead drawn to a picture. This one was big, perhaps 12 x 20 inches, the background soft in the style of the early 1940s, although the face remained tightly focused. He looked complete and confident, unaware his life wouldn't be measured through the long lens of old age, but as a brilliant, momentary flash.

Jack wondered when Wederbrook sat for the picture and guessed it was Shanghai, just before it all unraveled. Shanghai, where wild rickshaw rides past storefronts smelling of ginger root and roasted ducks was now a vanishing memory; where women, as if sensing the gathering turmoil, willingly shared their perfumed embrace before the spell broke and the unlucky Fourth Marines marched down Bubbling Well Road for the Philippines and then hell itself.

Jack turned from Wederbrook and joined Gladys, who'd found a place at the bar. He'd been so interested in the picture, he hadn't noticed much else. Now he looked around. A television pumped out its usual dismal racket that settled over a half-dozen bar patrons, each quietly straddling the gray side of middle age. For one who died in the adrenal rush of combat, being assigned permanent guard duty over such inactivity seemed demeaning, and it wouldn't have been unnatural for Wederbrook's framed face to sag over time.

"Anyone know the fellow in the picture?" Jack asked.

"Wederbrook," came a drawled out Panhandle reply. "First from here to die in the big war."

"Know how he died?"

That was a tougher question and the room grew thoughtful. No one in the place, maybe even in the whole town knew Wederbrook's story, how he died, or probably even why.

"I was there."

They circled up their chairs now, for this promised to be an unlikely Saturday diversion and there wasn't great carry to Jack's voice, even for one unloading a half-century burden. He waited until they'd gathered around him. Someone turned off the television.

"It was 1942 and we were stationed in the Philippines on the island of Corregidor," he began.

He described the soft phosphorous glow of Manila Bay and the splatter from Wederbrook's .30 caliber machine gun, how the barrel on those old weapons fired so hot they needed water cooling like a car's radiator.

Jack eased into the telling as an old man settles into a rocker, the memories suspended for a second before being pushed aside by another, each carrying him further and further, until the years melted off and he was 19 years old with hunger in his bones and a haunted look in his eyes.

"Ain't backin' up."

He told them parts of his own story because without one there is no other. There is context, color, shape, and the cordite smell of combat clinging to a foxhole.

There is Hanson, prisoner 995, and Johannsen, prisoner 996, appearing as if phantoms from the waves of shimmering Texas Panhandle heat. Good old reliable, big-hearted Hanson.

Once, during the worst of the afternoon artillery when the huge Jap pieces on Bataan and Luzon fired so regular that you could set your watch to it, Hanson plunked down into a sweaty cave on Corregidor's far side. The shelter was swamped with soldiers, protected from the rattling blasts above by a thick skein of dirt skinned over several feet of rock. The guy beside him casually thumbed through a *Reader's Digest*, ignoring the explosions, as if he were in a backyard hammock on some Ohio summer afternoon. Might as well relax, for no amount of talking, pleading, cussing, or praying ever altered the course of a determined artillery shell.

Like the guy with the magazine, Hanson figured he too was safe from all the bad angles, when amazingly, one renegade shell arched high in the cloudless sky that afternoon and lipped through the rim of the cave.

More than a dozen died outright in a blast that grew into a monster, sucking oxygen from their lungs and organs through their bones. It happened fast, in a second—dead, just like that. One moment reading a magazine, the next just dead. Amazing. When he recovered enough to think past the pounding in his ears, Hanson reached through the thick dust. His fingers came back sticky wet. The young soldier's arm, the one holding the *Reader's Digest*, was severed at the shoulder joint, exposing a leering gape of meat. Blood soiled his jungle uniform, spurting red rivulets onto the dirt floor where he lay. His face was fish belly gray, the color it gets just before punching out.

Hanson, good helping Hanson, unclasped his belt, cinched it into a tourniquet around the stump, heaved the soldier onto his back, stumbled over the bodies and up into the afternoon sunshine where shelling continued to flay the small tropical island. Out there somewhere beyond the blasts and dust was the Malinta Tunnel hospital. When the hot breath of artillery blew in their faces, Hanson dropped with a grunt to the hardpan earth and waited for it to pass. Soon he was exhausted. And terrified too. The bombed-out palm tree stumps splintered unevenly, offering no help from the flying rocks and killer metal. The armless soldier's blood-soaked shirt was a wet rag on Hanson's back.

It was nearly a mile to the tunnel, dodging fiery rips. For nearly a mile he carried the mutilated soldier, a boy not much older than high school friends back home. About 50 yards from the entrance to the Malinta Tunnel, an officer saw them and ran out to help. Minutes later, with all three tucked safe inside the dusty underground hospital, the officer ordered Hanson back out into the shelling. Hanson stared at him for a second in disbelief.

Hanson later learned that for his 50 yards of bravery, the officer won a Silver Star. Tunnel rats won medals; dogface privates just lost their arms. After that universal truth sank in, it brought a good laugh out in the foxholes when delivered with the proper twist of humor and indignation. Maybe the officer died with the medal on his chest in a Japanese prison camp. Hanson never cared to find out. Prison camp had a way of busting the pretensions some men spent lifetimes carefully building up. In that way, maybe it taught you something, another little fact you could use somewhere down the road, although the price of such lessons was steep.

Jack felt a gentle tug. He glanced at his wife and then his watch. More than two hours had passed. They'd spent enough time stirring up the dust around Wederbrook's grave. Jack's job was done.

Marine veterans who were prisoners of the Japanese have a saying: "Never buy green bananas."

What goes unsaid, but is understood by all, is you might not live to see them ripen. In that way they acknowledge, at least to each other, the toll of their experience.

When he looks backward, the war doesn't cipher much into the chronology of Jack's life, but it had a way of shaping everything. Those 40 months of captivity robbed him of at least a decade and it wasn't until somewhere near middle age before he felt caught up.

I look at it like it happened to somebody else. I can handle it that way. I look at it from the outside, I'm watching him.

When he first landed home, Jack was okay drinking beer with buddies, but mostly he was shallow-rooted, a sapling swaying in a dangerous Northwest blow.

Some drank. Some hustled every passing skirt because they could and it made up for lost time. Others outlasted the overseas prison camps only to kill themselves shortly after arriving home.

Jack's sister, Betty, was 13 years old when their mother pulled her aside and spoke the facts of it as clear as she could tell.

"Jack's taking a nap in there and he can't sleep without a gun or a knife under the pillow."

Sometimes before speaking, he froze and reformed words in his mind before some pidgin Japanese-English tumbled from his lips. And then when the voice inside cried like a child, he'd drift for weeks watching the miles eat away asphalt under his car tires. He was a kid running away to a secret hideout in the woods. He didn't consider the worry left behind. Just making up for lost time, that's all it was.

Once, shortly after the war, Jack drove all the way to Southern California through the lonely log-truck roads of Oregon, and when he pulled into Hanson's driveway, his old camp mate burst through the door with fire in his eyes.

"You're gonna' call home!" he ordered. Good old Hanson.

When he took on college at Gonzaga University in Spokane, he was doing fine until the day he stood before one of the classrooms shaking, for no outside reason, just shaking. Goddamn, it was awful. Who could blame a man for stretching asphalt between himself and his war.

For the briefest time in the summer of '47, he and another former prisoner immersed themselves in the business of selling used cars. It was easy money if you had the gift of pretending you cared.

They set up shop on the edge of Spokane's colored section and took off buying all the old 1939, '40, and '41 Buicks they could lay their hands on. The cars sat out front as yellow as canaries, all polished up with fender skirts and oversized white walls.

"Beat 'em and Cheat 'em," Jack announced into the black telephone in their rented office. "Cheat 'em speaking."

Eventually Jack worked into his own equipment-leasing business, bossing himself around instead of punching a time clock for someone else who just might remind him of a Mitsubishi shipyard honcho. Oh, the war changed him all right and in ways that weren't always visible.

What are you gonna' say to me, what you gonna' do that hasn't already been done?

He finished courting and married Gladys, a patient and good woman who worked hard at understanding, even when it seemed like too much trouble.

They settled in Everett along the shores of overcast Puget Sound, where they discovered how the sky can be painted a dozen shades of gray. It was as if Everett had been awaiting them all those years.

Gladys bore him a daughter, but it wasn't until their son Mike and then the grandkids arrived that he began to fully heal. Gradually he understood how in those early years he hurt everyone closest to him.

But he couldn't explain, even to his own family, the ways it burned.

One evening when Jack and Gladys returned to their Everett home, he thought he saw the shadow of movement inside. Something was amiss, perhaps an intruder. Jack slipped in and quickly doused the lights. If someone was in there, he didn't want them to see him either. Darkness evened the odds, buried the differences. Some part of that Yokohama prison warehouse would stay with him forever.

Even now he cannot sit in the daylight by an open window and watch the day unfold outside. In the light he's too obvious, too visible.

POW camp just after the Japanese surrender; Fran Agnes stands fourth from right, back row. Note sake bottles in front. "PW" was painted on barracks to notify American fliers where to drop supplies.

"I'm aware, too much aware," he said.

It's that way with the others as well. They plan for every situation and always look for the exits.

Although being from a generation that didn't complain, they learned to share their discomfort, the nightmares, the feeling of not fitting in. They gradually discovered that disconnection and anger burrowed deep into the marrow of most POWs. In a similar fashion, their longsuffering wives found comfort trading war stories of their own.

Galen and Henry, Fran and Odas, joined ex-POW groups. Talking, they learned, is a powerful salve. They found success and families that cared. They eventually moved to the Everett area, where middle age became old age.

Fran retired after 21 years in the Army. He worked for the Washington State Employment Security department for another 20 years after that. In 1981 he helped organize a local chapter of former POWs. Eventually he became national commander.

"I've had some real good years in my life. I don't focus on the POW years," he said. "When I took off that uniform, when I left the service that was the last day of my service. I started a new life. I don't focus back on camp life, the only time is when I go back to conventions and start reminiscing about 'when did *he* die and when did *he* die.'"

Henry Chamberlain prepares Veteran's Administration claims for other POWs, mostly World War II and Korean prisoners.

"I'm settin' myself up for some bad dreams tonight," he said once while recalling his days in Zero Ward.

Odas Greer stayed in the Army until 1957. Then he became a sewing machine repairman. In the early 1990s, he returned to the Philippines with his wife. They toured Corregidor, where he had nearly died 50 years earlier in the Japanese invasion.

Afterward, when they'd returned home, Odas told his wife: "I've completed the circle. Now I can forget it."

For his efforts during the war, Odas won two silver stars, two bronze stars, and two purple hearts.

"You can take 'em all down to the hock shop and get enough for a cup of coffee," he said. "Not that I don't value them, cash value don't mean a thing, but I *earned* them."

Raising the British and American flags for the first time at the POW camp where Fran Agnes was held. Flags were made from the parachutes that were used to drop supplies to the former prisoners.

Galen Martin retired from the military in 1961 and began working for Hughes Aircraft in California.

"I never let anyone bluff me after I came out of POW camp," he said. "I could meet any challenge there was out there."

While others of their generation eased into their final years, many of the POWs found purpose, a way of making something useful out of those lost years.

Fran, Galen, Jack, and the others regularly spoke to school children about a war so long ago. Jack has a box of homemade thank-you cards from Everett elementary students.

"We have to get it out of our system," Galen said. "You can't go around with it all bottled up inside of you. You have to have some recognition of what you did with your life, you can't push parts of it away. Speaking to the kids has been helpful. They have a lot of questions. The kids can't believe what happened. When we talk to kids it's like we have something to give."

Galen also became involved in helping feed the hungry.

"I know what it's like to starve."

They attend conventions around the country where they meet up with other former prisoners. Often at those conventions, middle-aged sons and daughters on personal reconnaissance missions move from table to table, white head to white head, quietly asking about their fathers. The children want to know what awful secret is hidden back during those lost years. They want to know what forces a father to wake up screaming in the middle of the night.

But there really are no answers. All that is left are stories—rattling bones from the lips of old men.

The house where Ed Fox lived for more than 70 years still guards one end of Wetmore Avenue. The nearby cherry and cedar trees grew so tall that their thick roots buckled the sidewalk—children and the elderly have to scale their concrete peaks when they pass.

Fox and his mother had arrived in Everett by train in 1914 and found themselves adrift in a waterfront village barely 20 years old. The place had high-masted fishing boats and wood-planked streets, and, when the tide ran out along the waterfront fully exposing its Puget Sound beachhead, the breeze carried a faint, lonely odor of the sea.

Everett seemed the farthest outpost in the nation, a place so damp moss grew on rooftops.

A mile southwest of the Fox house, the old Strand Hotel, anonymous and rundown as ever, stubbornly resists the changes around it. After the war, the hotel evolved into low-rent apartments with murky figures slipping in and out at crazy hours. Long past is the era of night clerks and Paine Field airmen bursting through the lobby on their way upstairs. But, in the same way it had during the war, the Strand survives.

A new brewpub sits directly across it on Colby Avenue. From a row of tables looking onto the street, you can sip a beer and look up into the open windows of the old hotel. Some nights figures move about inside, and you don't know if it's the effects of the beer or the power of the moment, but you can almost feel the building pulling you inside.

I was cozily parked in the overstuffed chair and reading a book, when suddenly the buzzer sounded. I looked at the board: 38 was ringing. I almost saw your ghost Gracie, damned if I didn't! But no Gracie there is in 38 any more, but a railroad man named Carry—a Norwegian, about 38 years old. I put down my book and went up, wondering what the hell he'd be wanting that time in the a.m. I knocked, and he immediately opened the door. "Yah," his deeply accented voice was saying. "Come in." I went in, glanced around for a moment at the old room. Turning about, I had a surprise. There sat Walt, with a glass in his hand, a big smile all over his face and way up to the top of his bald head. "Well Jesus Christ!" I exclaimed. Walt and Carry began laughing. Carry reached for a half-full bottle of Three Feathers whiskey. I reached for a glass, and was poured a stiff one. Walt and I got to kidding each other, heaving the b.s. around until the air was blue and Carry was laughing to beat hell.

"Remember the gal who used to be in this room?" I asked Walt. He smiled.

"Yes, by god, I'll never forget her. Grace was all right she was." He twirled his glass around for a moment, then added: "You know, I think Grace rather liked you, Ed."

I smiled, emptied my glass. "Possibly," I said, "possibly."—Ed

Dear Gracie, I'm awfully sorry, Gal, but on that watch business I can be of simply no help at all. I am rather in the dark about this whole business: not sure whether you lost the watch or that it was stolen. In the latter case, your chances of ever getting it back are pretty poor, regardless of how many marks of identification you could provide.—Ed

Dear Ed. Well I have some good news. I found my watch in a pawn shop. Had given up hope. It's been five months now. Have not gotten it yet but will soon I hope. Anyhow I know where it is. I would feel much better if I had it.—Gracie

Dear Gracie, So you finally found your little watch? Well, by god, I'm sure as hell glad to hear that. That's simply good luck—I did not think things like that ever happened anymore.—Ed

Ed Fox
Strand Hotel
Please send me $20 at once care Western Union.
Grace Emmett

The letters between Fox and Gracie dwindled to a trickle after the war, until they inexplicably stopped altogether in late 1948. It was as if whatever flash of middle-aged happiness that they shared in Everett had now seemed silly, or it just played out, when shined under the harsh spotlight of postwar life. Fox night clerked at the Strand another 14 years, but never again wrote to Gracie, who, for as much as anyone could tell, had disappeared off the earth.

His last fleeting words provide no clues.

Dear Gracie, How the old calendar does go round & round! Five years since you left this old burg… Well kid, we both hope this finds you well, & best wishes for the days to come.

Gracie's wristwatch remains to this day in a Seattle pawnshop—or at least it might. Fox eventually married a respectable Everett woman, divorced her a few years later, but kept writing even when she remarried. As Gracie could've told her, letters were his lifeline, books his truest love. Towards the end, the neighbors on Wetmore Avenue thought him a recluse. Fox died alone in 1993, a few weeks shy of his 90th birthday, surrounded by books piled so high his old rheumy eyes could barely see over them.

"It could eventually be classed as one of the finest libraries of its kind to ever come from the Pacific Northwest," gushed the Seattle bookseller who spent nearly a year driving to Everett to assess the 10,000 volumes in Fox's remarkable lifetime collection. Eventually, after months of sorting and organizing, the hardbacks filled 660 boxes and appraised out at $180,000. Fox wouldn't have cared about the money, one suspects, as long as his precious hardbacks found a proper home.

Jack stood alone at the Everett waterfront, his attention snagged on a fence of wooden piers exposed several feet out of the low tide muck. The old worn timbers were gnarled with clams and strands of dark green seaweed as far up as the washing tide could reach. It was a cold gray day, the kind that made him thankful for his overcoat. Dirty white seagulls with bright orange webs dipped and weaved, fighting an airborne dance over scraps on the beach.

To his back, behind a dirt bluff tangled with thorny blackberry bushes and wild grasses, stretched Everett and the memory of the small two-story house where a stray Army Air Corps P38 crashed more than 50 years earlier.

His mind wandered back. The cool day and the smell of seaweed reminded him unmistakably of the big warehouse barracks in Yokohama where his youth was torn from him. Hanson is there always and so is Johannsen and all the others, so bleak and barely existing.

At this same spot in Everett more than half a century earlier, a Navy shipyard with great skyscraping cranes poked through the harbor's pulp mill smoke. Today, nearly in the exact place, a modern multi-million dollar Navy base with looming gray warships once again protects Everett.

Jack looked at the pilings, and thought how in Yokohama he, Johannsen, and Hanson would've picked them clean and steamed those clams in their own juices. He could almost taste the raw, pulpy meat, could certainly see the dented metal bucket and the barren prison yard.

Johannsen died in 1997. His brother wrote, telling Jack that, strangely, when he'd visit his dying brother in the hospital, he'd find him cocooned in a fetal position underneath his blankets at the foot of the bed. It was just like at the prison camp all those many years ago.

Hanson died in the summer of that same year. It was a hard passing. In the end he didn't recognize much, wouldn't even have known Jack who understood him as well as a man had a right to. Galen Martin died in 1999. Odas Greer passed away in 2002, as did Fran Agnes in early 2003. It turned into a numbers game again, now with only a few left for roll call each morning.

Over the months and years of its telling, Jack's story tumbled out over cups of black coffee at his sturdy, wooden kitchen table. The big fir tree out back kept track of the passing seasons. On occasion, Jack's cat would paw at the door and he'd reach over, without breaking thought, and open the slider door. Sometimes he'd smile at a memory: Hanson, Johannsen, Walsh, Gaskin, and Greer.

"Do you see their faces, Jack?"

"Uh huh," he answers absently.

In his mind it is a cold bright winter day in Yokohama with his back propped against the wood barracks, his legs stretched-out stilts. Before him is busy Tokyo Bay, thick with Japanese warships. There are a few other prisoners with him, sunning themselves on a rare day off, trying to feel warm, which was impossible in winter with their thin wrapped rags. A sparrow landed close by on the dirt and Jack barely breathed, hoping it would hop closer. *C'mon, little birdie,* he thought, *please, please, please.* He was already dreaming of how it would taste in his watery soup.

Suddenly a tremendous explosion shattered the silence. Jack's head snapped back and his heart flayed madly for a second. But nothing more came of it and soon he realized it was probably just a ship's boiler overheating out there in the water. It seemed anticlimactic in a way, but still it was a lousy trick to the prisoners, who were jumpy beyond reason.

One of the prisoners sitting legs extended beside Jack pulled himself up and shuffled into the warehouse. Jack watched him disappear through the thinning sunlight. A while later, the last light streaked low over the Yokohama winter skyline, and Jack also retreated into the darkened warehouse, glancing at the prisoner now lying like a newborn on his narrow bay, enclosed in his coarse blankets. For the longest time no one bothered him. But after a while they grew worried. He wouldn't come off his bay, he just lay there with the blankets over his head. They tried coaxing him down with rice and soup, but he pulled the blankets ever tighter. For two days he lay like that. And then he died.

Jack still sees the blankets snugged around him. He imagines the face underneath, the tired jaw clenched, the eyes vacant and resigned. At that moment it could've been any of them.

He always sees their faces.

AUTHOR'S AFTERWORD

*n*early everyone who read drafts of this book wondered how I came upon the story. My answer was simple: I didn't come to it; it came to me.

I first heard of Jack Elkins one morning in 1995 when I was a reporter at the *Everett Herald*. Jack's son, Mike, appeared at the office that day with his father's story and a need to tell it. He asked for me.

I'd recently written about local people and their memories of World War II in Europe. Mike said I wasn't finished. He said I should also write about the war in the Pacific and, by the way, what did I know about the Japanese prisoners of war?

I was interested, but not entirely enthusiastic. At the time I felt ready to move on and explore other decades with different people and different histories.

Mike was insistent, however, his earnestness real. He said I should finish what I'd started. His father, he told me, had been a prisoner of that war. It was a hard, tragic, unbelievable story, he said. But in a strange way, it was also about hope.

Come, he said, and learn for yourself.

Into my hand he pressed a book about the island of Corregidor and the battle fought there at the start of the Pacific War. Read it, he said, and then you'll talk to my father. He turned and left.

On a loose sheet inside the book was his father's name, Jack Elkins, and his telephone number. That night I began to read.

Jack Elkins, on a Puget Sound shore, 1995. *Drew Perine, Everett Herald*

I found myself at Jack's kitchen table a week or so later, drinking coffee and carefully picking at the edges of his life. Jack was wary. I was cautious too, and still a little unsure of why I'd come.

I began scribbling notes on a large legal pad, but soon gave up and just listened as his voice seemed to shed years of rust. An hour passed and then another. The coffee grew cold. I realized it might be a story too deep and too complicated to ever understand.

Over the months, though, I found myself drawn to that kitchen table, Jack pouring coffee, turning down his radio, smiling at first with small talk, and then plunging in where he'd left off.

Listen, he taught me, for that is the beginning of understanding.

From Jack, the story began to branch out in ways I couldn't have imagined. I learned there were others like him who lived not far away, an odd brotherhood of the past. So I sought them out as well, for each POW has experiences to add. The Evergreen Chapter of the American Ex-Prisoners of War was helpful in my journey. As in all research, uncovering one layer leads to another, and another.

So I sat in the homes of other former prisoners or met them for long sessions in local cafes, stopping only to change tapes in my small recorder. Hours and hours of tape were needed to capture their personal histories. I was struck then, as I am now, about the clarity of their memories. For the most part, those events, the smells, the looks, the anger, and even the occasional, misplaced laugh is seared into their consciousness, even a half century later. There were days after interviews when I felt drained—I couldn't imagine their burdens.

And that brings me to Ed Fox and Everett. After the war, Ed's town grew into a city of 100,000 in a county of more than a half-million people. It still sits prominently on a peninsula pushed up between the Snohomish River to the east and Port Gardner Bay to the west. But now freeway traffic rushes past a downtown planned by great industrialists more than a century ago. Highway travelers blur by wide streets where solid brick mansions and flimsy wood whorehouses once stood, each taking something from the loggers and mill workers who made the town. They blur by the cedars and firs and fog that cling to the Snohomish River Valley on deep winter mornings.

"Slow down," I can almost hear Fox say, and see him behind the check-in desk of the old Strand Hotel. Waiting for Gracie.

In a file cabinet in the Northwest Room on the second floor of the downtown Everett Public Library, Ed Fox lives. I know, because I've seen his picture and heard him speak through the pages of his letters. I was in that room soon after this project began when I met up with Everett historian Dave Dilgard. I wanted to put some perspective on the story, I told him. I wanted to know what was happening in hometown America while the prisoners suffered overseas. My request was vague and still somewhat unformed in my mind.

"I may have something useful," Dilgard said and reached for a drawer containing the files of Ed Fox. The files were stuffed with the long, single-spaced letters Fox had written during the war. I later learned that Ed Fox was a pack rat of the first order. He kept carbons of virtually every letter he wrote. Thankfully, he also kept the letters he received from Gracie Emmett, and they became an important counterpoint in the telling of the Everett homefront story.

Fox was more comfortable in front of a typewriter than a telephone—when he died, files of letters and carefully clipped and indexed newspaper and magazine articles were piled about his small home on Wetmore Avenue. It was estimated that upwards of a half-million clipped articles were in that home.

Another piece of luck. Dilgard had actually interviewed Fox before he died, and could recall with great detail the nature of their conversation, the look and feel of the house, and the depth of his great curiosity and intellect.

Also fortunate is the fact that the World War II generation were letter writers and storytellers. Without those letters and the strength of their memories, this story never would have been told.

Sources

Primary

Ace Pursuiter. Paine Field, Washington, wartime newsletter.
Agnes, Fran. Recorded oral interviews.
Chamberlain, Henry. Recorded oral interviews.
Elkins, Jack. Recorded oral interviews.
Emmett, Gracie. Letters. Everett Public Library.
Everett Herald (Washington), 1941–45.
Fox, Ed. Letters. Everett Public Library.
Greer, Odas. Recorded oral interviews.
Martin, Galen. Recorded oral interviews.

Secondary

American Ex-POW National Medical Research Committee. "The Japanese Story," packet 10, July 1980.
Belote, James H. and William M. *Corregidor: The Saga of a Fortress*. New York: Harper and Row, 1967.
Daws, Gavan. *Prisoners of the Japanese: POWs of World War II in the Pacific*. New York: W. Morrow, 1994.
Hoyt, Edwin P. *Japan's War: The Great Pacific Conflict, 1853 to 1952*. New York: McGraw-Hill, 1986.
Knox, Donald. *Death March: The Survivors of Bataan*. New York: Harcourt Brace Jovanovich, 1981.
Mallonee, Richard C. *The Naked Flagpole: Battle for Bataan*. San Rafael, CA: Presidio Press, 1980
Miller, J. Michael. *From Shanghai to Corregidor: Marines in the Defense of the Philippines*. Marines in World War II Commemorative Series. Washington, DC: History and Museum Center, Headquarters, U.S. Marines, 1997.
Newsweek, August 1945.
Stewart, Sidney. *Give Us This Day*. New York: Norton, 1957.

Time-Life Books, editors. *Japan at War*. Alexandria, VA: Time-Life Books, 1980.

Toland, John. *The Rising Sun: The Decline and Fall of the Japanese Empire, 1936–1945*. New York: Random House, 1970.

Wernstedt, Frederick L., and J.E. Spencer. *The Philippine Island World: A Physical, Cultural, and Regional Geography*. Berkeley: University of California Press, 1967.

Wheeler, Keith. *Bombers over Japan*. Alexandria, VA: Time-Life Books, 1982.

INDEX